Editor
Dona Herweck Rice

Editorial Project Manager
Dona Herweck Rice

Editor-in-Chief
Sharon Coan, M.S. Ed.

Illustrator
Kevin Barnes

Cover Artist
Brenda DiAntonis

Art Coordinator
Kevin Barnes

Art Director
CJae Froshay

Imaging
Alfred Lau
Rosa C. See

Product Manager
Phil Garcia

Publishers
Rachelle Cracchiolo, M.S. Ed.
Mary Dupuy Smith, M.S. Ed.

W9-BHY-971

TRAITS
of Good Writing

Grades 3–4

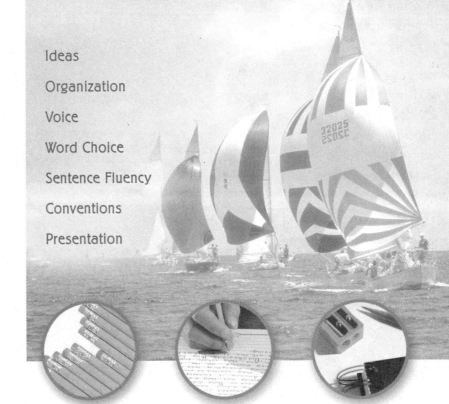

Ideas

Organization

Voice

Word Choice

Sentence Fluency

Conventions

Presentation

Author
Jennifer Overend Prior, M. Ed.
Reading passages provided by
TIME For Kids **magazine.**

Teacher Created Materials, Inc.
6421 Industry Way
Westminster, CA 92683
www.teachercreated.com
ISBN-0-7439-3282-X
©2002 Teacher Created Materials, Inc.
Made in U.S.A.

Teacher Created Materials

Table of Contents

Introduction

If you sit down and ask teachers what good writing looks like, they will say they know good writing when they see it. But what exactly is it that teachers look for when they read their students' work? Do all teachers look for the same qualities?

In the early 1980s, teachers in the northwestern United States felt they needed a set of common guidelines by which to teach and assess student writing. By comparing student writing that needed extensive revision to student writing that did not, certain characteristics—or traits—emerged. The qualities found in successful student writing have been revised over time and are now commonly known as the traits of good writing. Recently, in keeping with current academic standards that include communication skills, teachers are paying additional attention to the way a writing project is presented. These identified traits are listed and described below.

The focus of writing centers around its message, and in the **Ideas** section, you will find activities that help students to develop their themes so their ideas are clear and easy to understand. They will also learn how to provide interesting and useful details while avoiding the obvious.

Organization is also an important element of the writing process. In this section students learn how organization provides the skeletal support for the meaning of writing. Students learn to make connections to help the reader bridge one idea to the next.

Some say that the most difficult element of writing to teach is **Voice**, but it is essential that students grasp how they can make their words come alive with the resonance of their personalities. Voice is the connection we make with the writer that makes us want to continue reading.

In the section on **Word Choice**, students will learn how to use vivid, colorful, and dynamic words to enrich their writing and make it as precise as possible. They will also learn how to avoid trite language.

Sentence Fluency focuses on sentence variety, length, and the musical quality of words when they are placed near each other. The activities help students not only to recognize the rhythm and flow of language but also to use them in their own writing.

If writing does not follow the standard form in conventions, it can be very difficult to read and understand. The section on **Conventions** focuses on spelling, grammar, paragraphing, and punctuation. The activities take the students beyond worksheet learning and are student-centered, discovery-based learning tasks.

The final section, **Presentation**, is designed to help students incorporate visual material into their writing in order to emphasize their most important ideas.

Teachers need a variety of resources to help them support students in their journey toward becoming good writers. Look in any teacher's library and you will find many, many books about teaching writing. No single method of teaching is going to be a quick solution to problems in writing, but the lessons in this book are designed to give you solid ideas around which you can effectively instruct your students.

Brainstorming a List of Ideas

Objective

The students will learn the brainstorming technique as a way to gather ideas prior to writing.

Skills

- brainstorming
- identifying main idea
- identifying central ideas in an article
- identifying details
- planning a story
- writing a story

Materials

—chart paper

—black marker

—"Kids Light the Way" (page 6)

—student copies of "Author Ideas" (page 7)

—student copies of "Idea List" (page 8)

—"Student Writing Sample: Halloween Party" for teacher reference (page 9)

Procedure

1. Explain to your students that brainstorming is the process of thinking and exploring ideas about a topic.

2. Explain that sometimes, we make lists to record our ideas. Ask the students to tell about the reasons for which they have used lists in the past, such as grocery lists, to-do lists, etc.

3. Ask the students to select a topic for a class story. See the list below for ideas.

   - school event
   - activities on the playground
   - taking care of a pet
   - our teacher
   - our school
   - adventures in the cafeteria
   - adventures of a familiar book character

Brainstorming a List of Ideas *(cont.)*

4. After selecting a topic (such as activities on the playground) ask the students to brainstorm ideas about the topic as you write the ideas on chart paper. See the following example.

   Ideas: Activities on the Playground
   - kickball
   - four square
   - jumping rope
   - playing in the sand
   - playing tag

5. Beside each idea, have the students think of details to add, for example:

   four square: how to start a game, rules of the game, solving conflicts

6. Explain that once a list is made, it is easy to write a story using these ideas.

7. Read aloud the article on page 6.

8. Ask the students to tell the main idea of the article.

9. Distribute copies of "Author Ideas" on page 7.

10. Have the students think about the ideas the author may have brainstormed before writing. Then have them complete the page, using information from the article.

11. Ask each student to think of a topic for his or her own story.

12. Distribute copies of "Idea List" on page 8 for brainstorming. Then have the students use the lists to assist them in writing their stories.

Publication

1. Have the students work together to revise and edit their stories.

2. Encourage each student to illustrate his or her story for display.

Extension

1. Divide the students into pairs and have them work together to brainstorm ideas for a story. Then write the story together.

2. Arrange to have the students work with a class of younger children in your school. The students explain and demonstrate how to brainstorm ideas for a simple topic, such as, "What I did over the weekend." The students help the younger children to brainstorm ideas and then write a story.

Kids Light the Way

Firehouse gear is fascinating—shiny red trucks, tall ladders, long hoses. The Snyder brothers, Cory, 13, and Brock, 11, of Bowie, Maryland, get especially fired up about fire-fighting equipment. They bought $35,000 worth for the Bowie Volunteer Fire Department and are hot to help out even more.

The boys saw a story on the NBC TV program *Dateline* about an Oklahoma mother who raised $25,000 to buy a helmet called an IRIS (Infrared Imaging System) for her town's fire department. Its special goggles allow fire fighters to see clearly through smoke. It could have saved her three children, whom fire fighters couldn't find during a smoky rescue attempt.

"I just don't want anyone else to die in a fire like those three kids did," says Cory. He and Brock, both Boy Scouts, began a fund-raising campaign called Project Rescue Vision to raise $25,000 for an IRIS for their fire department.

With the help of about 50 kids, including their 6-year-old sister Makenzie, they sent approximately 10,000 letters asking for money from major corporations in and around Bowie. They met with business leaders. They even held raffles.

About four months later, on Fire Prevention Day in October 1996, the Snyders presented the IRIS to the fire department. A year later on Fire Prevention Day, they donated two SCBA (Self-Contained Breathing Apparatus) units and three gas monitors, which measure poison levels in the air. All that cost $10,000. Project Rescue Vision is working to raise $12,000 for the Jaws of Life, a device that helps fire fighters rescue people trapped in cars.

"Help out your community," urges Brock. "Get up and do something!"

Author Ideas

Think about the ideas the author may have brainstormed before writing the article, "Kids Light the Way." Complete the page below by writing details from the article below each heading.

Fire-fighting equipment

_____

_____

_____

_____

IRIS helmet

_____

_____

_____

_____

The boys' fund-raising project

_____

_____

_____

_____

Future fund-raising projects

_____

_____

_____

_____

Idea List

Use this page to brainstorm ideas for a story.

My topic: _____

Idea #1:

_____

Details:

_____

_____

_____

Idea #2:

_____

Details:

_____

_____

_____

Idea #3:

_____

Details:

_____

_____

_____

Idea #4:

_____

Details:

_____

_____

_____

Student Writing Sample: Halloween Party

The girls went to a Halloween party.

They were dancing and singing.

Linda went upstairs to put makeup on.

A clown scared her.

The girls ran away from the clown and ran home.

—Kenny W.

Ideas

Using a Word Web

Objective

The students will learn the clustering technique as a way to gather ideas and thoughts about a particular topic.

Skills

- clustering
- identifying main idea
- creating a cluster
- writing a story

Materials

—"She Takes the Cake!" (page 12)
—student copies of "Idea Cluster" (page 13)
—student copies of "My Ideal Job Cluster" (page 14)
—"Student Writing Sample: Mrs. G and the Giant Worm" for teacher reference (page 15)

Procedure

1. Discuss with your students the concept of clustering or creating an idea web.

2. Explain that this is a strategy for organizing ideas before writing. The ideas are first brainstormed. Then similar ideas are clustered together.

3. Explain that each cluster usually becomes a paragraph in a story.

4. Create a class cluster or web about a selected topic. For example, a cluster about baseball might look like the following:

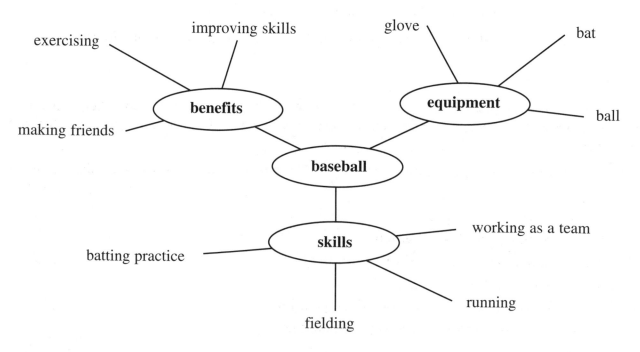

Using a Word Web *(cont.)*

5. Explain to the students that a cluster or idea web is a collection of ideas about a topic. The ideas are organized into categories. This makes writing a story much easier.

6. Read aloud the article "She Takes the Cake!" on page 12.

7. Have the students tell the main idea of the article.

8. Distribute copies of "Idea Cluster" on page 13 and have the students complete it by clustering the ideas in each of the article's paragraphs.

9. Next, have each student think about a job that would be ideal to have. See the list below for ideas.

   - athlete
   - dancer
   - author
   - computer programmer
   - game designer
   - chef
   - actor
   - veterinarian
   - artist

10. Ask each student to create a cluster using the outline on page 14.

11. After completing the cluster, ask each student to use the ideas to write a story about the ideal job.

Publication

1. Have each student illustrate his or her story.

2. Allow each student to read his or her story aloud to the class.

3. Assemble the students' stories into a class booklet for display in your classroom library.

Extension

1. Invite parents or community members to come to class to share information about their careers. Represent a variety of jobs, such as medical, veterinary, athletic, business, culinary, computer, and artistic careers.

2. Ask each student to interview a parent about his or her career. Have the student ask the following questions:

   - What is your career?
   - What do you like most about your job?
   - What kind of education is needed for this career?
   - What is most difficult about your job?
   - What special skills are needed in order to do your job?
   - If you could choose another career, what would it be?

She Takes the Cake!

For Claudia Fleming, life is sweet. She is up to her elbows in creamy custard and crumbling cookies all day long. At the end of the day, she is covered in powdered sugar and gobs of melted chocolate.

Sound delicious? Then perhaps Fleming has your dream job. She's a professional pastry chef. Her job is to create dozens of different, delectable desserts every day at New York City's Gramercy Tavern.

Her desserts must be ready for lunch and dinner, so Fleming starts her day at 7 a.m. and works until 9 p.m. But the long hours don't get her down. "It's like theater," she says. "You prepare all morning, and then the curtain goes up for lunch and dinner, and it's showtime."

Fleming, 40, has worked in restaurants for 15 years, but she wasn't always making desserts. She waited on tables, took cooking classes, and held other jobs before becoming an assistant pastry chef in 1990. "My job was to make life easier for the chef by weighing things and greasing and flouring all the molds," says Fleming. She was a good apprentice. She watched her boss carefully and pored over recipe books to learn the tricks of the trade.

For the past five years, she's been the one whipping up new desserts. Fleming recommends that future chefs read cookbooks and get a job in a restaurant. "Cook at home," she says. "Work any job in a restaurant and learn what the guests want."

The best part of her job: "You produce something that you can smell and touch and taste," she says, "and then you make someone happy with it."

Idea Cluster

Complete the cluster using the information from the article "She Takes the Cake."

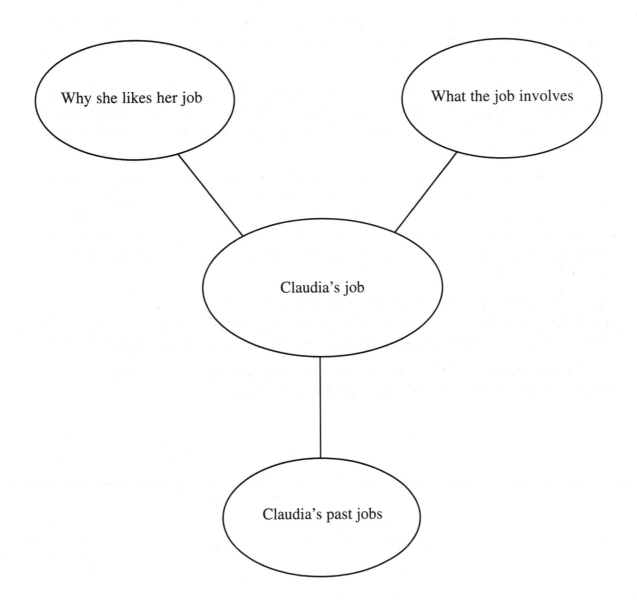

My Ideal Job Cluster

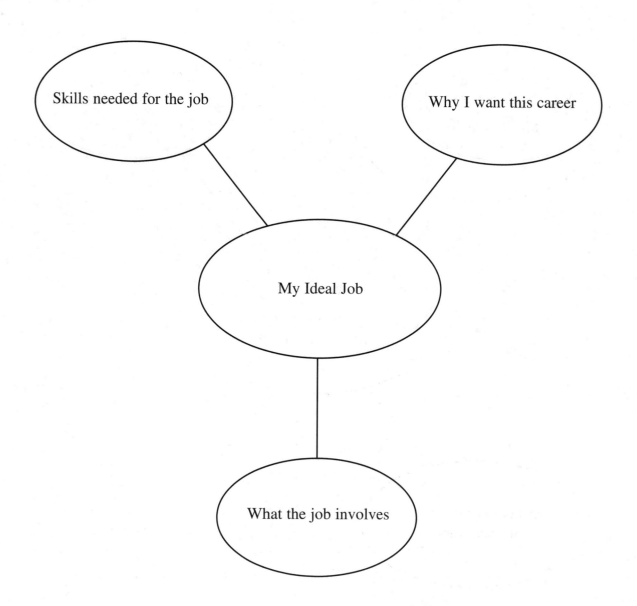

Student Writing Sample:
Mrs. G and the Giant Worm

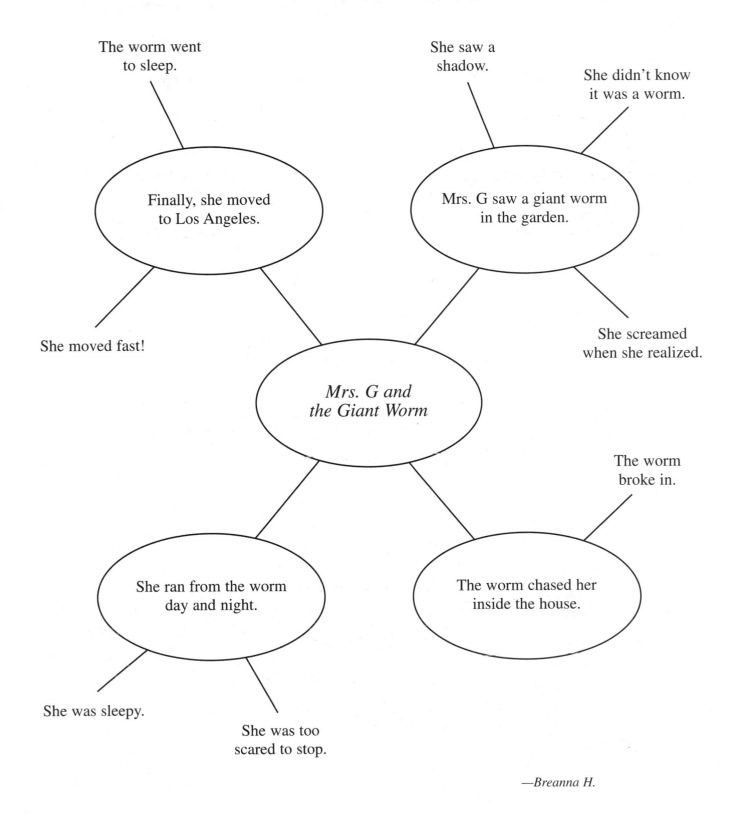

The worm went to sleep.

She saw a shadow.

She didn't know it was a worm.

Finally, she moved to Los Angeles.

Mrs. G saw a giant worm in the garden.

She moved fast!

She screamed when she realized.

Mrs. G and the Giant Worm

The worm broke in.

She ran from the worm day and night.

The worm chased her inside the house.

She was sleepy.

She was too scared to stop.

—*Breanna H.*

Story Planning with an Outline

Objective

The student will plan a written piece using an outline.

Skills

- understanding how an outline is used
- planning a story with an outline
- outlining a story
- writing a story from an outline

Materials

—chart paper
—marker
—"The Friendliest Firehouse" (page 18)
—student copies of "Using an Outline" (page 19)
—"Student Writing Sample: Story Outline" for teacher reference (page 20)

Procedure

1. Explain to the students that an outline is a tool for constructing a story or a report. It is used as a guide for the writer in order to assist with planning what will be included and how it will be organized. An outline also helps the writer to plan details that will be included in the story.

2. On chart paper, write the basic outline format below.

    I.
        A.
            1.
            2.
        B.
            1.
            2.

3. Explain that when making an outline, Roman numerals, capital letters, and numbers are used. Define the use of each in the following way:

    I. Main ideas
        A. Fact or subtopic of the main idea
            1. detail about the fact or subtopic

4. Provide the following example. If a person wanted to write a story about a pet dog, the author might want to tell about the animal's behaviors, routines, and training needs. The author would begin the outline by planning the paragraph about behaviors. See the following sample outline.

    I. My Dog's Behaviors
        A. Likes to Play
            1. runs around the house
            2. chews on her toys
            3. bothers the cats
        B. Likes to Sleep
            1. naps on the couch
            2. snuggles in my lap

Story Planning with an Outline *(cont.)*

5. Draw the students' attention to the outline's layout. *Behaviors* is the main idea. *Playing* and *sleeping* are listed as behaviors and each has a set of specific details related to it.

6. Read aloud the article "The Friendliest Firehouse" on page 18. As a class, create an outline to show how the author organized the main ideas, subtopics, and details of the article.

7. Distribute student copies of "Using an Outline" (page 19).

8. Have each student select a topic about which to write. The student writes three main ideas about the topic after the Roman numerals and then writes the subtopics and details beside the capital letters and numbers.

9. Finally, ask each student to use his or her outline to write a story. Point out to the student that each Roman numeral section will be its own paragraph.

Publication

1. Divide the students into pairs to read each other's stories. Encourage the students to compare the stories to the outlines and check to see that all main ideas, subtopics, and details from the outline were included in the story.

2. Display students' completed stories along with their outlines.

Extension

1. Show the students how to create an *outline* using a word-processing program. In Microsoft Word, open a new document and then click on the *View* menu at the top of the screen. Select *Outline*. The student can type an outline and it will be formatted accordingly. Using the *Tab* key on the keyboard will indent lines and place them in boldface type.

2. Provide the students with a list of story ideas. (See below.) Instruct each student to plan his or her story using an outline.

   • How to Make Spaghetti
   • What My Parents Should Know about Having Fun
   • Things I Like to Do
   • The Best Way to Solve a Math Problem
   • How to Plan for a Camping Trip
   • How to Play Soccer

The Friendliest Firehouse

Chicago firefighter Lieutenant Arthur Lewis studies the coloring books three girls have proudly placed before him. Whoops! A few crayon marks stray outside the lines, and a firehouse dog is colored purple. But it's a good effort, and Lewis rewards the girls with quarters. Now they can buy supper—a "poor man's" sandwich and fries—at Harold's Chicken Shack down the street.

Suddenly, a siren wails. The girls know the drill. They walk calmly out of the firehouse as Lewis and other firefighters grab coats and helmets. One slides down the brass pole from upstairs, and the crew is out the door in a blink.

The firefighters of Engine Company 16 battle blazes in one of the nation's poorest neighborhoods. But when they are off duty, they open their doors and hearts to local kids.

Ten years ago, Engine Company 16 was a hot spot for crime. Firefighters often came back from an emergency to find smashed windows and missing equipment at the station house. Frustrated, the firefighters just quit locking up. Soon, students from nearby Hartigan Elementary School began to drift through the open garage door. They used the bathroom, got their bikes fixed, or just hung out.

There was one problem: the kids were visiting during school hours. Lewis came up with an idea. With extra cash from the firehouse pay phone, he bought a few small radios. Kids who showed an improved school-attendance record would win a radio. The result? Last year, Hartigan's attendance rate shot up to 94%, one of Chicago's highest.

The firefighters realized they could do even more for the kids. Al Shaw, who drives the fire truck, now teaches chess at the kitchen table. Steve Ellison cuts kids' hair, and Andre Raiford helps with math homework. Other firefighters collect winter clothes for the kids. Some have started baseball and basketball leagues. Many firefighters are there even when they aren't working. Engine Company 16 has changed from a troubled firehouse to a safe home base for hundreds of kids.

Jeremy Woods, 9, drops by to play football and stand on the fire truck. "They tell me to stay away from drugs and to stay in school," he says. "It's my favorite place to come."

Using an Outline

Plan a story using the outline below. When outlining, remember the following things:

- Write main ideas beside the Roman numerals.
- Write subtopics beside the capital letters.
- Write details beside the numbers.

   I. _____

    A. _____

        1. _____

        2. _____

    B. _____

        1. _____

        2. _____

  II. _____

    A. _____

        1. _____

        2. _____

    B. _____

        1. _____

        2. _____

 III. _____

    A. _____

        1. _____

        2. _____

    B. _____

        1. _____

        2. _____

Student Writing Sample: Story Outline

I. Main characters

    A. Felicity

        1. very smart

        2. loves to horseback ride

    B. Penny

        1. saving the day

        2. is ridden every day

    C. Grandfather

        1. always knows what's best

        2. knows a lot of things

II. Setting

    A. King's Creek Plantation

    B. Woods

III. Problem

    A. Ben runs away and stays in the woods.

        1. He has no food and no water.

        2. Two men are coming to get him.

        3. Ben doesn't know two men are coming.

IV. Resolution

    A. Felicity comes to save Ben.

        1. Felicity brings Ben food.

        2. She brings Ben home.

V. Favorite part

    A. Felicity finds her horse.

—Jordyn A.

Writing Enticing Leads

Objective

The student will write a creative lead to attract a reader to read his or her article.

Skills

- identifying a lead
- understanding what makes a good lead
- writing a lead to attract a reader's attention

Materials

—"After the Spill" (page 23)

—chalkboard

—chalk

—student copies of "Interesting or Not?" (page 24)

—student copies of "Lead Me On" (page 25)

—"Student Writing Sample: Crazy Day" for teacher reference (page 26)

Procedure

1. Explain to your students that the first sentence of an article can be very powerful. After reading the first sentence, the reader makes a decision whether or not to continue reading the article. It is important that the first sentence of an article catches the reader's attention, piques curiosity, and draws the reader into the story.

2. Read the first sentence of the article "After the Spill" on page 23. (See below.)

   Four minutes after midnight on March 24, 1989, a dark poison began to spread through the waters near southern Alaska.

3. Ask the students to discuss their feelings about the sentence. Ask the following questions:

   - What spread in the waters?
   - Where did this happen?
   - What do you think the "dark poison" was?
   - What feeling does this lead sentence give you?
   - Does this sentence make you wonder what the article is about?
   - What questions does this sentence bring to mind?

4. Explain to the students that an interesting lead sentence captures a reader's attention. Does this lead sentence capture your attention? Does it make you want to read the article?

5. Read the remainder of the article.

6. Write the following lead sentence on the chalkboard:
   This story is about an oil spill.

Writing Enticing Leads *(cont.)*

7. Tell the students that this is a very common type of lead sentence, but it does not capture a reader's attention. This kind of lead sentence tells what the article is about, but it does not give the mysterious feel that is created by the lead sentence in "After the Spill."

8. Explain that there are many ways to begin a lead sentence. Write the following lead starters on the chalkboard:

   • Imagine that . . .

   • Have you ever (seen, wondered about, tried, etc.) . . .

   • What if . . .

9. Tell the students that these kinds of leads create interest and draw readers into the story.

10. Distribute copies of page 24. If the lead is interesting, the student writes "yes." If the lead is not interesting, the student rewrites it to make it interesting.

11. Have student pairs compare their leads, discussing the ways they tried to add interest to the leads.

12. Have each student select a topic about which to write.

13. Distribute copies of page 25. The student writes his or her topic and then uses the lead starters to write several different leads. The student then selects one of the leads to use for the story.

14. Ask each student to write a story about his or her topic.

Publication

1. Display the students' completed stories on a bulletin board entitled, "Take the Lead."

2. Encourage students to read each other's stories, focusing on the leads used.

Extension

1. Display a list of uninteresting leads on your classroom computer. Allow the students to write interesting leads below each one. Have the students italicize the new leads.

2. Have each student create a list of lead starters to store in his or her writing notebook. Encourage the student to review the lead starters for use in future stories.

3. Distribute copies of children's magazines. Ask the students to look for articles and read the lead sentences. Which lead sentences capture their attention? Which ones stir up emotions? Which leads are not very interesting?

After the Spill

Four minutes after midnight on March 24, 1989, a dark poison began to spread through the waters near southern Alaska. Millions of gallons of black oil gushed into the sea. The oil was pouring from a giant oil tanker, the *Exxon Valdez*. It had crashed into rocks in Prince William Sound.

Terrie Williams, a marine biologist, was called to the scene. Dead fish littered the shore. Birds hopped about helplessly, their feathers gooey with oil. Sea otters tried to clean themselves by licking their filthy fur. No one knew how best to help these animals. "It was total chaos," Williams recalls.

Williams and other volunteers set up an emergency hospital for oily sea otters. Their first patient was a teenage otter they nicknamed "Fred Jr." Williams helped scrub him for two hours with soap and water.

Fred Jr. was the first of hundreds of otters to be treated by Williams and her team. Some lived; many did not. The spill killed nearly 3,000 sea otters, including Fred Jr. It also killed more than 250,000 seabirds, 300 harbor seals, 250 bald eagles, and as many as 22 killer whales. Billions of fish, clams, oysters and other small sea creatures also died.

Many years and many dollars were spent cleaning up the oil spill—the worst in U.S. history. Even though the cleanup was completed in 1992, scientists continue to study the area. A government group in Alaska released a report on life 10 years after the spill. The good news: "There has clearly been a lot of recovery," says Molly McCammon, who heads the government group. The not-so-good news: "For several species, such as harbor seals and killer whales, and the ecosystem in general, there is a long way yet to go."

A region's ecosystem is its community of plants and animals. Within an ecosystem, each living thing depends on other living things for survival. Fewer fish mean less food for seals. Fewer seals mean less food for killer whales. Humans are part of the ecosystem too. Many Alaskans depend on fish and seals for food and income.

The *Exxon Valdez* accident was deadly, but some good came of it. The government bought thousands of acres of coastal and forest land in the area to protect the animals there. And experts now understand much more about handling this kind of disaster. Terrie Williams believes this knowledge could help save creatures caught in future oil spills. "We could take a lot better care of Fred Jr. today than in 1989," she says. "We've learned a lot since then."

Interesting or Not?

Read each lead sentence below. If the lead is interesting, write "yes." If the lead is not interesting, rewrite it.

_____ 1. This article is about my pet.

_____

_____

_____ 2. The sky opened up with a thunderous roar.

_____

_____

_____ 3. Have you ever been so excited that you thought you would burst?

_____

_____

_____ 4. This story is about a parade.

_____

_____

_____ 5. I went on a vacation.

_____

_____

_____ 6. My report is about cats.

_____

_____

_____ 7. Imagine that you woke up one day and you couldn't see the sun.

_____

_____

_____ 8. Once upon a time, there was a girl.

_____

_____

Lead Me On

Write the topic of your story. Use the lead starters to create interesting leads for your story.

Topic: _____

Imagine that . . .

_____

_____

Have you ever . . .

_____

_____

The most fascinating thing . . .

_____

_____

It all started when . . .

_____

_____

Did you know . . .

_____

_____

What if . . .

_____

_____

Student Writing Sample: Crazy Day

Amelia woke up to a strange noise. She turned over to look at her alarm. It read 5:30. "UGHHH!" she groaned. "Jimmy, If that's you down there, please stop. Some people like to get a little sleep on their weekends." She called down the hall, still laying in her bed, "Then again," she mumbled, "you probably don't even know what the word sleep means." The weird noise kept on going. "Jimmy, I mean it!" The noise played on. "I'm telling mom and dad!" Amelia cried.

Just then, Jimmy walked in, his hair sticking up, and him looking very groggy. "What's with all the racket, Sis?" her 9-year-old twin brother asked, groaning.

"I thought it was you," Amelia said.

"Nope," answered her brother.

"Uh-oh. Mom and Dad are gone on vacation. Who, *or more importantly,* what *is making that noise?"* she thought.

"I'm gonna go check it out," said Jimmy, walking toward the door.

"NOOOOOOOOOOOOO!" Amelia screamed. When she did this, Jimmy stopped, and so did the noise, for a second. When it did this, Amelia thought she might have scared off whatever it was. But after pausing for a moment the thing started howling away again.

"What's your problem?" her brother asked, still a bit startled from the yelling.

"Well," she started, still a bit embarrassed by her outburst, "what if it's some dangerous wild animal? You prancing down the stairs towards it would be a pretty easy target," the girl, said.

"Yeah, and some helpless-looking 9-year-old girl lying in bed screaming at the top of her lungs isn't an easy target," mumbled Jimmy. Amelia rolled her eyes, but the fear inside of her forced her to walk over to the door and shut it. She tried to look casual as she did this, but the fear also caused her to sit in a chair where she could climb up to her top shelf. After sitting for a while, her brother finally said, "No use sitting here thinking about all the bad things that could happen. Let's go!"

She agreed, but said, "We'll have to go secretly and quietly. They crept down the stairs very secretly, and *extremely* quietly.

"I think it's coming from the couch," said Jimmy.

Amelia listened for a moment. "I think your right," she agreed. She realized how much calmer she felt with her brother close by. Without him, she probably would've been lying in a big pile of nervous tears on the floor. With this in mind, she crept bravely with her brother to the back of the couch. The noise was louder, much louder. For a moment, Amelia thought she recognized the noise, but she couldn't think of anything like it at the spur of the moment. Jimmy put his hands slowly over the edge of the couch. Amelia was about to do the same, but a picture of some wild beast biting off a little girl's hands stopped her from doing so.

Her brother peered over the edge. His face held a look she had never seem him make before. She winced. What did he see? A ferocious tiger? A clever fox? An unknown creature? Suddenly Jimmy fell to the ground, laughing so hard Amelia really did think his head would fall off. "It's, HAHA, just, HEHE, her! HOHOHOHO!"

"What in the world?" thought Amelia. She looked over the edge. There sat their babysitter, snoring away. She fell beside Jimmy, who was still laughing. *That's* where she had heard that noise before—her dad! She smiled. *"What a crazy day,"* she thought.

–Chloe F.

Transitions and Sequencing

Objectives

The student will sequence a personal narrative with a beginning, middle, and end. The student will include details to create visual images.

Skills

- identifying beginning, middle, and end
- identifying central ideas in an article
- identifying details
- planning a story
- writing in proper sequence
- writing a story

Materials

—"Fire! Fire!" (page 29)

—student copies of "'Fire! Fire!' Sequence" (page 30)

—student copies of "My Personal Narrative" (page 31)

—"Student Writing Sample: *Mrs. G and the Giant Worm*" for teacher reference (page 32)

Procedure

1. Explain to your students that all narratives have a beginning, a middle, and an ending. The story is incomplete without these elements.

2. Read aloud "Fire! Fire!" on page 29.

3. Discuss the article. Allow the students to share their feelings about the story.

4. Explain to the students that the beginning, middle, and end of a story includes specific elements.

   Beginning
   - describes who is involved
   - describes where the event happened
   - describes about the problem

   Middle
   - describes what happened

   End
   - describes how the conflict is resolved

5. Explain that the story about the fire was written in a specific sequence. Ask the students what would happen if the events of the story were rearranged. Would it change the meaning of the story?

6. Number the paragraphs of the article randomly and then read the article aloud in the order that you numbered the paragraphs.

Transitions and Sequencing (cont.)

7. Invite the students to respond to the article read in this manner. Was it difficult to understand? How important is sequencing when writing a story?

8. Discuss the original article. What events happened at the beginning, in the middle, and at the end of the story?

9. Distribute copies of page 30. Ask the students to complete the page by categorizing the paraphrased events—beginning, middle, end.

10. Next, divide the students into small groups. Ask the groups to share stories of events that have happened to them.

11. Instruct each student to select a personal experience story to write about.

12. Before writing, have the student create a list of details about the experience. Explain that, at this point, it is not necessary to write the events in order.

13. Distribute copies of page 31. The student sequences the story ideas by writing whether the events should be at the beginning, middle, or end of the story.

14. Have each student use this page to assist in writing the personal narrative.

Publication

1. Allow the students to share their completed stories.

2. Display the students' stories along with their planning pages.

Extension

1. As a class, write about a recent school event. Before writing, brainstorm a list of major events and details to include in the story. Then determine the sequence of ideas. Have pairs of students work together to write stories about the event. Then allow the students to share their stories, comparing the sequence of events and details.

2. Divide students into groups of two or three. Have students, in turn, share a personal story. After the storytelling, the other group members write the story they heard, carefully sequencing the information.

Fire! Fire!

Mom always says I have a good sense of smell. One night last November, I smelled smoke. Then I heard a fire engine. My heart turned into a huge drum. Was our building on fire? Mom grabbed her keys and we ran outside.

The fire engine was in front of the building next door. Smoke was coming from a window in front. More and more fire engines came, but we didn't see any flames or fire. We just saw lots of people who lived there come out. Although it was cold out, one woman had only a blanket thrown over her jeans and shirt.

Mom and I went home because we were getting cold. A few minutes later someone knocked on our door. When I opened it, I found a firefighter standing there. I was speechless! He looked huge! He had his firefighting clothes on, with that big hat and boots and a belt full of tools that clanked when he walked. He was smiling, though. When Mom came to the door, he was still smiling, but he was very firm. "Put on your coats, please," he said. "Turn off anything on your stove. You need to leave the building immediately."

Our building was not on fire, he told us. But the fire next door was serious. His fire engine company from the nearby town of Skokie had come to take charge of our building. So it was his job to make sure that we were all safely out.

Mom and I looked at each other. "Can I gather some things?" Mom asked him. I could tell she was a little scared. "No, ma'am," he said, very politely. "You need to come with me NOW. Are there just two of you who live in this apartment?" "Yes," we told him as we got our coats. He walked us down the stairs. He wouldn't let us take the elevator. He told us to join the crowd across the street and not come any closer to the building. He went back in.

Now we could see flames coming out of the roof next door. The Skokie fire truck was in the alley, spraying a huge fountain of water on our roof. We later found out this was to keep our building from catching fire. Thank goodness, it worked.

Mom had grabbed her purse and portable phone. She called my older sister. Anne was frantic. She had heard about the fire on the television news! Her husband Steve came to get us. The firefighters wouldn't let us get our car from the garage.

In the morning, we all went to see what had happened. The building next door had burned down. There wasn't much left of it except a couple of back walls. Several fire trucks were still there. Luckily, everyone had gotten out safely. A firefighter told us we could go back into our apartment.

The people who lived in the building that burned lost everything. They were never allowed to go back in. That woman who had only a blanket over her jeans when Mom and I first went out that night? She never even got to go back for her coat.

The first thing people in my building did when we went home was to put all new smoke alarms in the halls and in our apartments. We didn't need the firefighters to remind us, and trust me, we'll never forget.

"Fire! Fire!" Sequence

Read the events below. Write the sentences on the lines indicating which events happened at the beginning, middle, and end of the story.

- I heard a fire engine.
- Everyone got out safely.
- Some people lost everything.
- The building next door was on fire.
- The firemen were spraying water on our roof.
- I smelled smoke.
- We put new smoke alarms in the apartment.
- Mom called my sister.
- A fireman said we had to leave.

Beginning

_____

_____

_____

Middle

_____

_____

_____

End

_____

_____

_____

My Personal Narrative

Brainstorm a list of ideas for your story.

_____

_____

_____

_____

_____

_____

Sequence your ideas.

Beginning

_____

_____

_____

Middle

_____

_____

_____

End

_____

_____

_____

Student Writing Sample:
Mrs. G and the Giant Worm

One day Mrs. G was working in her garden when she saw a different shadow behind her.

"Oh, hi, Mr. G!" she exclaimed.

She was not aware that there was a giant worm right behind her that she was calling Mr. G. Well, it took her just about an hour to figure out that there was a giant worm right behind her.

Once she figured it out, she screamed! That worm was just about a mile away when she got into her house. The worm didn't care. He broke into the house. Well, that worm had chased Mrs. G right back outside. Day and night, sleepy-eyed Mrs. G kept running.

Then the worm went to sleep. This gave Mrs. G time to escape. So, she packed and left. She decided to move to Los Angeles. When she told her family about this, they freaked out. So, they all moved to Los Angeles. They all dyed their hair black. That worm also decided to look for Mrs. G in Los Angeles, but it didn't find her. So, she said goodbye to the worm and lived happily ever after.

—Breanna H.

Writing Dynamic Conclusions

Objective

The student will write a conclusion that summarizes written work in an intriguing way.

Skills

- identifying the criteria of a conclusion
- understanding how to make a conclusion dynamic
- understanding the effectiveness of a good conclusion
- planning a conclusion
- writing a conclusion for a story or report

Materials

—"By the Numbers" (page 35)

—chalkboard

—student copies of "Dynamic Conclusions" (page 36)

—student copies of "Writing a Conclusion" (page 37)

—"Student Writing Sample: Strange Cologne" for teacher reference (page 38)

Procedure

1. Explain to the students that the conclusion of a story is as important as the body of the story. It helps the reader to summarize the information read and holds the reader's interest right up to the end.

2. Discuss the following elements of a conclusion:
   - begins with a summary statement
   - addresses the main ideas of the story
   - relates to the introduction

3. Read "By the Numbers" on page 35. Ask the students to pay particular attention to the conclusion.
   - Does it begin with a summary statement?
   - Does it address the main ideas of the story?
   - Does it relate to the introduction?

4. Next, explain that a conclusion can systematically address each of these elements or it can be dynamic. That means that it is unique and captures the reader, leaving a lasting impression of the story.

5. Discuss the following additional elements that make a conclusion dynamic.
   - connects the story to a personal experience
   - addresses ideas beyond the story
   - challenges the reader to think or take action
   - leaves the reader wondering what will happen next

Writing Dynamic Conclusions *(cont.)*

6. Read the conclusion of "By the Numbers" again.

7. Identify the elements of the conclusion that make it unique. For example, the first sentence of the concluding paragraph uses alliteration. This means that several of the words begin with the same letter: "Toliver's wacky ways work wonders!" The author uses this technique to hold the reader's attention.

8. Write the following sentence on the chalkboard:

   And that means she'll have another trick up her sleeve tomorrow!

9. Explain that this sentence makes the reader wonder what the teacher might do next.

10. Provide each student with a copy of "Dynamic Conclusions" (page 36). The student completes the page by identifying dynamic sentences used in conclusions.

11. Instruct the students to write stories with dynamic conclusions. Provide a copy of "Writing a Conclusion" (page 37) for each student to plan the conclusion. This page assists students in thinking about their audiences and purposes for writing as well as planning sentences that restate main ideas and include dynamic elements.

Publication

1. Divide the students into pairs and have them evaluate each other's story conclusions. Have the students review each other's planning pages as well as the written conclusions.

2. Display the students' stories on a bulletin board entitled, "In Conclusion . . . ."

Extension

1. Have each student read a magazine article, paying particular attention to the conclusion. Ask each student to evaluate the author's ability to summarize and review the main ideas. Then have the student respond to the author's ability to engage the reader by connecting to personal experience, challenging the reader, or causing the reader to wonder what might happen next.

2. Instruct each student to select a piece of written work from his or her writing portfolio. Ask the student to evaluate the conclusion and then rewrite it in a way that is dynamic and captures the interest of the reader.

By the Numbers

A creepy vision in white slowly entered the classroom. It was a mummy, bandaged from head to toe. The students weren't scared, though. They had a feeling it was really their incredible teacher, Kay Toliver. She was simply dressed for the occasion. Halloween? No—a lesson about shapes, like pyramids.

Toliver uses all sorts of unusual tactics to teach fourth- through sixth-graders to solve real-life problems with math. She even had them race Tinkertoy cars to teach them how to calculate speed. "You can learn while having fun," says Toliver, a teacher at New York City's East Harlem Tech/Public School 72 for 33 years.

Now millions of TV viewers can learn math while watching Toliver's antics on *The Eddie Files*, a PBS program she hosts. A fictional main character named Eddie uses Toliver's math lessons to solve his everyday challenges. He used her lesson on speed, for example, to calculate the fastest route to catch a lost dog.

Unlike Eddie, an actor who's heard but never seen, Toliver and her students are real people. The kids don't get a grade for the videotaped summer sessions, but they do become math wizards. And they get to be on TV. The show also introduces real workers who describe how they use math in their jobs.

Toliver's wacky ways work wonders! A study of more than 500 students in four U.S. cities recently showed that their math skills multiplied after tuning in. Toliver says her greatest gift isn't fame or the educational awards she and the show have won. "It's when students get that 'I got it' look in their eyes, then share with the class," Toliver says. "That means learning is taking place." And that means she'll have another trick up her sleeve tomorrow!

Dynamic Conclusions

Read the concluding paragraphs below. Underline sentences that are unique and capture reader interest. Write a letter beside each paragraph to identify the dynamic element used in the conclusion.

A—connects the story to personal experience

B—addresses ideas beyond the story

C—challenges the reader to think or take action

D—leaves the reader wondering what will happen next

1. Fancy was headed for her stall, and I couldn't stop her. The barn door opening was coming up FAST, and it looked mighty small. I held my body close to Fancy's neck and buried my face in her mane as we raced into the barn. If she'd had brakes, they would have squealed as she slid into her stall. I turned around to a laughing Uncle Jim and said, "I'm ready to go again!"

2. People who are afraid of bats have burned them out of caves or buried them inside mines or under city construction sites. "They think every bat is a vampire bat, and they kill all they can find," says Thomas Kunz, a Boston University biologist.

3. An air supply would also be needed. But with the right equipment, people can live in strange places. "We have a year-round base in Antarctica," says Boyce. "Today's kids may end up living on the moon."

4. "Help out your community," urges Brock. "Get up and do something!"

5. The *Exxon Valdez* accident was deadly, but some good came of it. The government bought thousands of acres of coastal and forest land in the area to protect the animals there. And experts now understand much more about handling this kind of disaster. Terrie Williams believes this knowledge could help save creatures caught in future oil spills. "We could take a lot better care of Fred Jr. today than in 1989," she says. "We've learned a lot since then."

Writing a Conclusion

Use this page to plan a conclusion to a story you have written.

Reviewing Information (for planning purposes)

• The audience and purpose for writing:

_____

_____

• Main ideas of the story:

_____

_____

• Conclusion:

　　—Summary statement:

_____

　　—Restating the main ideas:

_____

_____

　　—A sentence or two addressing personal experience, challenging the reader, or creating
　　　curiosity:

_____

_____

_____

Student Writing Sample: Strange Cologne

Bobby walked into The Pizza Palace. It was his favorite restaurant. It had a playland, video games, and most of all, great pizza. Max waved to him as he walked in. Max was one of the workers and a great storyteller.

"Where have you been?" asked Max.

"Oh, I was on a vacation for the past week. Why?" Bobby answered.

"Haven't you heard? He's still recovering!"

"Recovering? Recovering from what?" Bobby asked.

"Sit down, sit down and I'll tell you the whole story," Max answered.

"It was Monday afternoon and we were all doing our usual work. Then he walked in."

"He? Whose he?" Bobby interrupted.

"Wait, wait! Let me finish!" Max scolded. "We greeted the newcomer and asked his name. He asked us please to call him Nick. He had the strangest smelling cologne on. No one really thought of it as strange, though. The next day everyone started acting strange. You know how Jo always gives good advice? Well, anyway, I was standing in the kitchen when I heard little Jenny walk up to Joe. She told him that she wanted to get her ears pierced, but her parents wouldn't let her. Then Joe told her that she should go get a needle and do it herself!"

Bobby was so astonished, he didn't say a word, but sat their with his mouth hanging open.

Max went on, "Also, you know how the co-workers, Sara and John, always fight? Well, they came in on Wednesday holding hands. I thought that was very odd. I asked Sara to come help me. She said, "Okay. This will only take a sec, honey," and gave John a smooch on the cheek! Just as she did this, Joe walked in. "Sara!" he exclaimed. "What are you doing?"

"What do you mean?" he asked. "Isn't it okay to give your fiancé a little kiss?"

Joe looked like he was going to faint. "Fiancé!" he exclaimed.

"Yes, we're getting married tomorrow. You will come to the wedding, won't you?" She just smiled. "Well, tata!" she called and they walked off together.

They weren't the only ones acting strangely. Everyone who was around Nick was acting odd. The funny part was, no one noticed how funny they were acting, only how others were acting. The next day Nick walked in. He looked normal until he saw how strange everyone was acting. He then jumped up and yelled, "Ha ha! It has worked! You were all tricked by my new invention! Cologne that takes over brains! It worked on you! Then he ran out the door."

"Weird!" Bobby exclaimed. "What did you do?"

" Well, I took them to the doctor who gave them medicine and told them to rest a while.

"Wow!" Bobby said. Max got up and was about to leave when Bobby said, "Wait! Why weren't you affected by the cologne?"

"Well, because I slap floor," he answered.

"What?"

"I slap floor," he said and walked off. Just then, Joe walked in.

"Joe!" Bobby exclaimed. "Are you alright?"

"What?" asked Joe. Bobby told Joe what Max told him, including the 'I slap floor' part.

"I slap floor, I slap floor," Joe repeated. "Oh, I know," he finally said. "Think about it, Bobby. Today is the first day of the fourth month of the year. Now, still thinking of that, write down the words 'I slap floor,' and try to unscramble them. They will make two words," he said.

–Chloe F.

Writing for a Particular Audience

Objective

The student will use knowledge of the audience to appeal to the audience's emotions and interests when writing.

Skills

- understanding and appealing to the audience
- writing for a particular audience

Materials

—"A Girl Named Rockett Takes Off" (page 40)

—student copies of "Analyzing the Audience" (page 41; two for each student)

—student copies of "Focus on the Audience" (page 42)

—"Student Writing Sample: What All Kids Should Know About Their Parents" for teacher reference (page 43)

Procedure

1. Ask the students to brainstorm different groups of audiences. Student responses may include mothers, fathers, students, teachers, athletes, babysitters, police officers, girls, boys, etc.

2. Read aloud page 41, "Analyzing the Audience."

3. Instruct the students to keep these questions in mind as they listen to you read "A Girl Named Rockett Takes Off." As you read the article, pause periodically to discuss the clues the author gives about knowledge of the audience.

4. Have students complete the reproducible in response to the article.

5. Ask the students to find specific places in the text that show the author is using his or her knowledge of the audience.

6. Have the students select a topic for writing. Have them complete another copy of "Analyzing the Audience" to anticipate the needs of the intended audience.

Publication

1. Divide the students into pairs and have them listen carefully to each other's stories. They can compare their work to page 41 to determine if they met the needs of the intended audience.

2. Post the students' stories on a bulletin board display. Have each student draw a picture to represent the intended audience. Post the illustration beside the story.

Extension

Distribute copies of "Focus on the Audience" (page 42). The students will practice writing about the same topic for different audiences.

A Girl Named Rockett Takes Off

Just when eighth-grader Rockett Movado was making friends at her new school, she faced a sticky situation. She was invited to two parties on the same day. What should she do? That's for you to decide—if you happen to be a girl.

Rockett is the star of CD-ROM games produced by Purple Moon, a company in California that wants to make computer games more fun for girls. For years, game software was primarily designed with boys in mind. Purple Moon is just one of several companies now targeting girls. It seems to be working. In the past year alone, sales of computer games for girls have grown from $26 million to $64 million.

In the new game *Rockett's Tricky Decision,* there's nothing to shoot and no piling up points to set a new record. The goal of this game is to make decisions that help Rockett deal with school, friends, and her feelings.

"We do research with girls all over the country," says Nancy Deyo, president of Purple Moon. "We find out what they think about, what their bedrooms and their friends look like. That's how we create Rockett's world." Purple Moon did four years of research before producing its first game. The company found that girls are as eager as boys to play computer games, but girls seem to prefer games that have lifelike characters and stories.

Some kids think that making some games especially for girls is unnecessary. But since girls have different interests yet still like to play computer games, the Rockett games fill a real need. Anyway, boys are welcome to enjoy the games, too. Lately several have sent e-mail asking permission to be on the Purple Moon Web site (*http://www.purple-moon.com*). "Of course, we let them visit," says Deyo. On the Web site, Rockett fans can play games and exchange postcards. If you're looking for good games that involve real-life situations, check out the Web site. Then try one of Rockett's adventures yourself.

Analyzing the Audience

Respond to the following questions in order to get to know the audience. Use this worksheet as a guide before you begin to write.

1. What is the age and gender of the intended audience?

   _____

2. What is the audience's highest level of education?

   _____

3. Where does the audience live (city, country, house, apartment)?

   _____

4. What are the audience's interests?

   _____

5. What kind of setting does the audience appreciate?

   _____

6. What kind of person does the audience appreciate?

   _____

7. Which elements of style will be particularly appealing to the reader?

   _____

8. What does the audience already know about the topic?

   _____

9. What does the audience want to know about the topic?

   _____

Focus on the Audience

Pretend that you have decided to convince people at school that lunch recess should last longer. Write a persuasive paragraph to each of the audiences below. When writing each paragraph, be sure to write in a way that would appeal to that audience.

Teachers:

_____

_____

_____

_____

_____

_____

Students:

_____

_____

_____

_____

_____

_____

Principal:

_____

_____

_____

_____

_____

_____

Student Writing Sample: What All Kids Should Know About Their Parents

Here are all the reasons parents tell us what to do or, for that matter, tell us not to do. For instance, why do they always make us eat vegetables all the time? Sure they say it's because they're good for you and it is true that they're healthy, but the real reason they make us eat those little greens is because if we don't eat our veggies, they'll soon take over the world!

Fingernails—why can't we bite them? It makes them look ugly? Yes, but the real reason is that if our nails stay down to stubs for too long, they will disappear completely.

Chores, chores, chores, so many chores! Why do we have to do them? Everyone needs to do their part in the family? Sure, but do you want to know the real reason? It's because if kids don't do any work at all for a long time, they'll become paralyzed in their arms and legs.

Screaming can be fun, but we're never aloud to do it. Why? It's annoying and it hurts people's ears? True, but do you want to know the real reason? If you scream too loud for too long, your head will soon fall off. That's right. It'll fall clean off.

How do I know all this? Hmm . . . I'm not sure. Why haven't they ever told us about this? Hmm . . . I don't know that one either, but don't get me wrong. I'm not trying to make it so you won't trust your parents. I'm just trying to warn you that when they tell you to do, or not to do something, obey them. They may have even better reasons than what they say.

—Chelsea F.

Experimenting with Voice

Objectives

The student will identify the voice in a narrative. The student will write in different voices.

Skills

- brainstorming
- identifying voice
- using a distinct voice
- discriminating between voices

Materials

—chart paper
—marker
—"What a Winter!" (page 46)
—student copies of "The Author's Voice" (page 47)
—student copies of "Speak Up!" (page 48)
—student copies of "Finding Your Voice" (page 49)
—"Student Writing Sample: Aliens" for teacher reference (page 50)

Procedure

1. Explain to your students that when reading an article, it is possible to get a feeling about who the author is and how he or she feels about the topic.

2. To demonstrate the use of different voices, ask two students to tell about the same event. (Have one student cover his or her ears or leave the room while the first student speaks.)

3. Have the students compare the two stories. Then ask the following questions:
   - Did the students tell about the same event?
   - Did they tell the exact same story?
   - Did they both feel the same way about the event?
   - Who liked the event more?
   - How would you describe the students' feelings about the event?

4. Continue to explain that when we tell a story verbally or in writing, we use a certain "voice" that reflects our feelings and opinions.

5. Write a topic, such as *a rainy day*, on chart paper. Then write a list of "voices" such as:
   - teacher
   - parent
   - kid
   - tree
   - car washer
   - umbrella maker

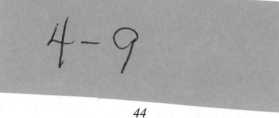

4–9

Experimenting with Voice *(cont.)*

6. Ask the students to discuss how each would respond to a rainy day. Draw the students' attention to the fact that each has a different response to the same topic.

7. Select one of the "voices" in step 5 and write a class narrative about a rainy day from that perspective. Write sentences contributed by students on chart paper. For example, a teacher might dread a rainy day, knowing that the students will not have recess outdoors and will be highly restless during class. A person who washes cars for a living might be upset because no one will come in to get his or her car washed. On the other hand, a flower would be happy to have a fresh drink of water, and a young child might be excited about the prospect of splashing in puddles.

8. Read aloud "What a Winter!" on page 46.

9. Ask the students to determine the voice of the author. How does he or she feel about the topic? What message is the author trying to communicate?

10. Distribute copies of "The Author's Voice" on page 47 and have each student complete the page by answering questions about the article.

11. Next, distribute copies of "Speak Up!" on page 48. Have students determine the different voices that could be used to tell the story.

12. After completing the page, have each student select one of the voices on the planning page and write a story from that perspective.

13. For future work with identifying the author's voice, have students complete "Finding Your Voice" on page 49.

Publication

1. Have students work together to revise and edit their stories.

2. Allow the students to word-process their stories, using a font to reflect the voice used.

Extension

1. Have each student write about a special person he or she knows or knows about. For example, the student may choose to write about a bully in the neighborhood, a sports figure he or she admires, or a special family member. Encourage the student to use words that express his or her feelings about the selected person.

2. Provide copies of several children's literature books that are written from the first-person point of view. See the list below. Ask the students to read one of the books and then write a summary of the story, describing the main character's "voice" and how the character feels about what happens in the story.

Suggested Literature

I Was a Second Grade Werewolf by Daniel Pinkwater

The Tenth Good Thing about Barney by Judith Viorst

The Relatives Came by Cynthia Rylant

What a Winter!

The Ewen family awoke to a scary sight: a nearby creek was spilling over its banks. Soon the rising waters surrounded their Guerneville, California, home. The Ewens escaped by wading through knee-deep water.

"I didn't expect it to come up that fast," says Melissa Ewen. The last time she and her children saw their home, it was nearly covered with water. "Everything we own was in there—photos that can't be replaced."

During the winter of 1997–1998, strong winter storms slammed much of the U.S. While bad weather often hits at this time of year, a change in climate patterns called El Niño made these storms even more dangerous than usual.

El Niño caused strange weather worldwide. Said James Baker of the National Oceanic and Atmospheric Administration: "This is the weather event of the century."

Heavy rain began to pound California on February 1. The rain triggered flash floods and mudslides. Forty-foot waves crashed over beaches. Fierce winds knocked out power to thousands of families.

At the same time, thunderstorms and tornadoes roared across Florida, tossing around trees, roofs, and even small parked planes. Winds gusted to 100 miles an hour.

Snow, rain, and wind battered much of the East Coast as the storms moved north.

Much of this wild weather was predicted by scientists who study El Niño. El Niño is a natural shift in the way winds and ocean currents travel across the Pacific Ocean. It happens every few years.

El Niño turns the world's weather topsy-turvy. Some countries that usually receive a lot of rainfall may suffer from droughts, while heavy rains and flooding often surprise other areas. This El Niño was the most powerful of the century.

El Niño affects more than weather. It warms up large bands of water in the Pacific Ocean, and this confuses many living things. Tropical fish and birds travel too far north. Sea lions in California starved because the fish they eat swam south.

El Niño was at its strongest in December, but much of the world felt its effects for months to come.

The Author's Voice

Use the article "What a Winter!" on page 46 to answer the questions.

1. What can you tell about the way the author feels about El Niño?

   _____

   _____

   _____

2. List the words used in the article that express emotion (such as *scary*).

   _____

   _____

3. The author uses strong descriptions to show amazement about the strength of the storms. For example, "Thunderstorms and tornadoes *roared* across Florida, *tossing* around trees, roofs, and even small parked planes." Write three other sentences from the article that use strong descriptions.

   _____

   _____

   _____

   _____

   _____

4. What message is the author trying to communicate through this article?

   _____

   _____

   _____

Speak Up!

Imagine that there was a huge snow storm overnight. Different people will feel different ways about the storm. Write a list of different voices that could respond to the snow storm.

_____

_____

Select one of the voices above and write a story about the snow storm from this voice.

_____

_____

_____

_____

_____

_____

_____

_____

_____

_____

_____

_____

_____

_____

_____

_____

_____

_____

Finding Your Voice

Use the graphic organizer below to analyze the author's voice.

Remember that voice is the way the author writes about a subject that reveals his or her personality as well as his or her beliefs or feelings about the subject.

Topic: _____

Audience: _____

Purpose: _____

Words, sentence, or passage from the text:

_____

_____

_____

_____

Author's feelings on the topic:

_____

_____

_____

_____

Are the author's feelings about the topic consistent throughout the text?

_____

_____

_____

_____

_____

Student Writing Sample: Aliens

"I will never go to Earth," Alien Tiny shouted.

"Oh, yes, you will, even if I have to put a leash on you," replied Alien Mom.

"Precisely. You have to," exclaimed Alien Smart.

The aliens lived on Uranus and were traveling to Earth.

"We need to parent-nap the parents and bring them back to Uranus. Then with the extreme machine, we will turn them into aliens."

Alien Mom barked. The aliens stepped into the time machine and were off. When they got there, nobody was outside. It was just them.

"Let's burn down the houses," Alien Smart said.

The only problem was that it wouldn't work.

"I hate being a bad alien," Alien Smart exclaimed.

"Yeah, me, too!" shouted Alien Tiny.

"Forget it," Alien Mom said.

Then they flew back to Uranus.

—Breanna H.

Narrative Voice

Objective

The student will write a story using narrative voice.

Skills

- understanding narrative voice
- writing from personal experience
- including words in writing that reveal personality and emotion

Materials

—article, "The Great Pumpkin Hunt" (page 53)

—chart paper

—marker

—student copies of "Narrative Voice" (page 54)

—"Student Writing Sample: Winter Break" for teacher reference (page 55)

Procedure

1. Explain to the students that voice refers to the way an author writes. The voice used by an author reveals his or her personality and feelings about a topic. There are different kinds of voices used in writing. This lesson focuses on the voice used in narrative writing.

2. Read aloud "The Great Pumpkin Hunt" on page 53.

3. Ask the students to discuss the article. Whose voice is expressed? Lead their discussion with the following questions:

   - Who is telling the story?
   - Why are they frustrated?
   - What is the mystery?
   - Does the author share personal feelings?
   - What were you able to learn about the author's personality?

4. Draw the students' attention to the personal nature of the story. The way the article is written gives the reader the feeling that he or she is with the author while the story is happening.

5. In "The Great Pumpkin Hunt," the author even asks questions as if addressing the reader: "Now what would we do?" "Where was she taking us?"

6. Explain that narrative voice is personal. It usually involves a person telling a story from experience. We are often able to sense the author's emotions.

7. Read the article again and ask the students to identify words used in the story that express emotion. (See below.) Write the students' responses on chart paper.

   - laugh at their silly faces
   - we slouched home
   - Dad grumbled
   - we had a blast
   - it's supercalifragilisticexpialidocious

Narrative Voice *(cont.)*

8. Distribute copies of "Narrative Voice" on page 54. The students will use the page to plan personal narrative stories.

9. After completing the page, have each student write a story of a personal experience. The student uses the planning page as a guide.

10. Encourage the student to write in a way that expresses emotion and reveals his or her personality.

Publication

1. Have students work in pairs to discuss their narratives. Have student pairs respond to the following questions:

    • What emotions or feelings were expressed in the story?
    • What words were used to express feelings?
    • What visual images were created in the story?
    • Were you able to identify with the story?

2. Post each student's narrative on a bulletin-board display. Above each narrative, have the student post a word that expresses the general emotion of the story. For example, the author of "The Great Pumpkin Hunt" might post the word *confusion* or *excitement* above his story.

Extension

1. Provide magazines and newspapers for the students to read. Instruct them to find examples of narrative writing. Ask the students to identify examples from the narrative articles that reveal personality and/or emotions.

2. On your classroom computer, display a personal narrative. Have each student read the narrative and use the underline tool to identify words that express the emotions or feelings of the author.

The Great Pumpkin Hunt

It was just pumpkins we were looking for that October Saturday. We were searching for ordinary pumpkins that we could carve into fantastic jack-o'-lanterns. We wanted to laugh at their silly faces. We wanted lots of them to decorate our front porch.

My brother Tim and I went to the supermarket, where we usually get pumpkins every year. They said they only had some baby ones that were too small to carve.

Now what would we do? We slouched home, wondering whether Mom or Dad would have any ideas. Dad said he would take us for a ride to see if a roadside vegetable stand had some pumpkins. "I can't believe they won't," he said. "It is October, after all."

So we piled into the car and drove out of town. The vegetable stand Dad remembered wasn't there! And we didn't see any others, either. Dad grumbled that he couldn't figure out where the farmers were selling their vegetables these days. By that time, you can imagine how Tim and I felt. Maybe we wouldn't have any jack-o'-lanterns this year.

I guess Mom knew the minute she saw us that we had been unsuccessful. But she said we should all just come with her. This time she drove. Where was she taking us? A secret pumpkin store? She seemed to know exactly where she was going.

As she turned the car into the parking lot of City Hall, we saw a Farmers' Market. Wow! This is where all the farmers brought their vegetables! There were hundreds— no, thousands—of pumpkins. Huge ones, tiny ones, medium-sized ones. We'd never seen so many pumpkins to choose from!

We splurged some allowance money on the biggest one we'd ever had. We got some ordinary-sized ones, too. Even Dad and Mom helped carve them. We had a blast. And our porch is not just fantastic for Halloween—it's supercalifragilisticexpialidocious!

Narrative Voice

Plan a narrative about a personal experience. Use this planning page to write a story.

Story topic: _____

Where did the story take place? _____

Who was with you? _____

What happened?

_____

_____

_____

_____

What feelings did you have?

_____

_____

_____

_____

What happened that was funny, exciting, scary, etc.?

_____

_____

_____

_____

How did the experience end?

_____

_____

_____

_____

How did you feel at the end?

_____

_____

_____

Student Writing Sample: Winter Break

I had a great winter break! I had Christmas at my house this year. We usually have it at my grandma's house. We also had Christmas at Mom's house, too. We usually have it at my Nana's house. I got lots of things like money and a safe from my dad. I put my Christmas money and small Christmas toys in it.

Something else I did over winter break was I played with my friend Lindsey. We had a lot of sleepovers! It was very fun! We played Pictionary and soccer. Lindsey and I love soccer! We play it every day. I had a magnificent winter break!

—*Lindsey W.*

Expository Voice

Objective

The student will write using expository voice.

Skills

- understanding expository voice
- identifying factual information in a text
- differentiating between expository and narrative voice

Materials

—"Dino Eggs by the Dozen" (page 57)

—student copies of "Understanding Expository Voice" (page 58)

—student copies of "Narrative or Expository?" (page 59)

—"Student Writing Sample: Reading" for teacher reference (page 60)

Procedure

1. Explain to the students that voice refers to the way an author writes. The voice used by an author often reveals how he or she feels about a topic. There are different kinds of voices used in writing. This lesson focuses on the voice used in expository writing.

2. Read aloud "Dino Eggs by the Dozen" on page 57.

3. Ask the students to discuss the article. Lead their discussion with the following questions:

   - What is the author's purpose?
   - Was the author personally involved in the event?
   - How does the author feel about the story?

4. Draw the students' attention to the fact that the author is conveying information. Even though we know that the author is interested and excited about the discovery, we also know that the author is relaying information.

5. Point out to the students the author's use of the third-person point of view.

6. Distribute page 58 and have the students complete it with information from the article.

7. Remind the students that personal narrative writing is written from the author's standpoint. Have them complete page 59 for practice with identifying different types of voice.

Publication

Instruct each student to write an expository piece to convey information about a selected topic. Ask the student to underline specific facts used in the piece.

Extension

Fill a folder with a variety of narrative and expository articles. Ask the students to select articles to read and identify the voice used.

Dino Eggs by the Dozen

More than 70 million years ago, a group of female dinosaurs roamed along a riverbank in South America. They had chosen the area as a place to lay their eggs—thousands of them! One by one, the baby dinosaurs started to hatch.

Then a giant flood washed over the land. The dinosaur nursery was lost forever.

Well, not quite forever. In November, 1998, a group of scientists announced that they had uncovered the buried nursery. They found it in Patagonia (Pat-ah-go-nee-uh), a dry region in Argentina.

Scientists working there saw a field covered with rocks the size of grapefruits. They took a closer look: the "rocks" were really dinosaur eggs. "There were thousands of eggs all over the place," says Luis Chiappe, one of the team's leaders.

The eggs belonged to long-necked, plant-eating dinosaurs known as sauropods (sore-u-pods), a group that included giant Apatosaurus (a-pat-o-sore-us). A smaller sauropod called a titanosaur (tie-tan-o-sore) probably laid these eggs.

Of course, a "small" sauropod wasn't very small. An adult titanosaur was more than 50 feet long. Newly hatched babies were about 15 inches long. "That's the size of a small poodle," says Chiappe.

The flood buried the eggs in mud. The mud helped preserve the remains of the babies still inside the eggshell. One egg contained 32 teeth, each small enough to fit inside this capital "O." Others contained fossilized patches of scaly skin.

Chiappe and his team returned to Patagonia. They hoped to answer more questions, including whether the mama dinosaurs made careful nests or laid their eggs just anywhere. With so many eggs yet to be studied, those answers may just be waiting to hatch.

Understanding Expository Voice

The author of "Dino Eggs by the Dozen" writes to convey information to readers. Write several of the facts the author includes in the story. Then tell how the author feels about the discovery.

Facts in the Article:

1. _____

2. _____

3. _____

4. _____

5. _____

6. _____

Author's feelings about the discovery:

_____

_____

_____

_____

_____

_____

Words or phrases used to express the author's feelings:

_____

_____

_____

_____

_____

_____

Narrative or Expository?

Read each passage and decide if the voice used is narrative or expository. Write *N* if it is narrative. Write *E* if it is expository.

_____ 1. When large numbers of people began settling in Florida nearly a hundred years ago, the Everglades were considered worthless swampland. Builders did their best to drain the swamp. Farms and cities sprang up where alligators once roamed freely.

_____ 2. When I was a kid in Arizona, I loved going to the state fair to see the dancing, sand painting, and displays of rugs and jewelry of the Navajo people. These days the Navajo hold their own Navajo Nation Fair every September. I was thrilled to be able to go last year.

_____ 3. Before you say I was crazy or foolish, just hear me out. My brother Patrick is six years older than I am, and even when he was 11 he knew everything about nature. He used to tell me about where snakes go in the winter and why rabbits wiggle their noses and how hippos can hold their breath for such a long time under water. So it was not too surprising that when he told me about two creatures I'd never heard of before, I believed him without question.

_____ 4. It's a giant squid, one of the earth's most mysterious animals. No one has ever seen a live giant squid. Scientists have been able to study only a few body parts that have washed up from the ocean over the years.

_____ 5. This mysterious burial room in the Pyramid of the Moon was discovered by scientists working in the ancient city of Teotihuacan in Mexico. They hope the room will help them figure out who built the city and its pyramids.

_____ 6. When I walked into the kitchen, I knew something was wrong. There was an odd rustling noise. It sounded like a critter quietly pushing objects around. Mouse! A mouse in the house!

Student Writing Sample: Reading

Reading is lots of fun. By reading you can travel to faraway lands, go back in history, or take a trip to the future. When you read you are in a totally different world of your own. There are all sorts of books in the world. Lots of people have their very own libraries. And, of course, there are plenty of public libraries in the world. A lot of schools have their own libraries or they have book mobiles (libraries on wheels) that come once a week for a few hours so the children can check out books. You could find books on almost anything. Of course, there are dictionaries, thesauri, and encyclopedias, but there are also books about individual things. There are books about history and books about famous people. There are books full of short stories and there are books with only one certain story. There are learning books and teaching books, complicated books and simple books, long books and short books. There are lots of different types of books. If you ever want to find something out, go to a library.

—Brody P.

Descriptive Voice

Objective

The student will use descriptive language in writing.

Skills

- understanding descriptive voice
- identifying descriptive words and phrases
- rewriting text to add descriptive language
- writing original stories using descriptive words

Materials

—"The Poetry Express" (page 63)

—chart paper

—marker

—student copies of "Jazz it Up!" (page 64)

—student copies of "Descriptive Language" (page 65)

—writing paper

—pencils

—"Student Writing Sample: Christmas" for teacher reference (page 66)

Procedure

1. Explain to the students that authors use different types of voice in writing. The author's voice conveys purpose, feeling, and personality.

2. Continue discussion by explaining that some authors use a descriptive voice. This means that they use language that helps the reader to form visual images or picture what is happening. Descriptive voice utilizes adjectives, powerful verbs, and detailed descriptions.

3. Read aloud "The Poetry Express" on page 63. As you read, have the students listen for descriptive words or phrases that help them to create visual images of the story. (See below for examples in the article.)

   - jazzy
   - catching the eyes of commuters
   - rushing to board a train
   - people pause
   - a new crop of poems sprouted

4. Explain that the article could have been written informatively and accurately without the descriptive language. It is the use of descriptive words and phrases that makes the article more interesting to read.

Descriptive Voice *(cont.)*

5. Write the following passage on chart paper:

   Commuters have been able to see new signs in subway stations in Washington. Instead of getting on the train right away, people read poems written by kids. In spring, new poems were placed on city buses.

6. Ask the students to compare this passage to the article. They will likely notice that the descriptive language was removed and that the passage is informative, but not very interesting to read.

7. You may even want to extend this activity by having the students offer suggestions for more descriptive words that can be added to the article to make it even more interesting.

8. Distribute copies of "Jazz it Up!" on page 64. The students complete the page by rewriting a passage, adding descriptive language.

9. Next, provide each student with a copy of "Descriptive Language" on page 65. On this page, the student changes each word or phrase by making it more descriptive, using more interesting adjectives, powerful verbs, or visual images.

10. After completing the page, ask each student to write a story about an experience. The student may use words or phrases created on the "Descriptive Language" page or create new ones to include in the story.

Publication

1. Allow students to share their stories with classmates. Encourage discussion on the use of descriptive words and phrases. You may want to post the following questions to guide their responses to the stories:

   - What interesting adjectives did you hear/read in the story?
   - What powerful verbs did the author use?
   - What parts of the story helped you to create visual images?

2. Display students' stories on a bulletin board entitled, "Picture This!"

Extension

1. Allow students to review stories in their writing portfolios. As students reread their stories, ask them to add descriptive words to increase visual imagery and to add interest for readers.

2. Invite students to word-process their stories on your classroom computer. Show the students how to italicize or boldface descriptive language used in the stories.

3. Instruct students to create a folder of writing ideas. One of the pages in this folder should be devoted to descriptive language. On this page, each student writes descriptive words and phrases found in books and magazines. Encourage the students regularly to add to this page and refer to it when writing their own stories.

The Poetry Express

Jazzy new signs in subway stations have been catching the eyes of commuters in Washington. Instead of rushing to board a train, people pause to read poems written by kids.

The lighted posters, called Metro Muse, are at 10 train stops in the busy city. On display: 12 thoughtful compositions to celebrate kids' creativity and promote reading.

Writer Laurie Stroblas began the District Lines Poetry Project in 1994, hoping to give bus riders something better to stare at than ads or graffiti. She had been leading poetry workshops in public schools, so she asked her students to lend a hand.

"The response was incredible," says Stroblas. Last year she decided to transfer her idea to the subways and picked new poems with the advice of 150 students. Organizations donated enough money to keep Metro Muse in subway stations all winter. In spring a new crop of poems sprouted on city buses.

What are the poems about? Snow falling, the arrival of a new year, love, fear, and peace. Cindy Rosales, a sixth-grader at Oyster Elementary School, was inspired two years ago by her favorite type of music: "Kindness is the jazz," she wrote. "Bring the big jazz in/The big/whole jazz."

Like most poets, the kids had mixed feelings about letting the public read their private thoughts. "I would feel glad that someone read my poem," one girl said. "But I would feel sad if they missed their train."

Jazz it Up!

Rewrite the paragraphs below. Add at least three descriptive words. You many use the Word Box below to help you.

Sleeping with the Dinosaurs

When it was time to set up our "camp," I knew just what to do. I decided we would bed down under the apatosaurus. Its ribcage overhead would look cool in the beam of my flashlight.

People were scattered on the floor around us. The sounds of voices echoed in the halls. Moonlight streamed in through a window.

_____

_____

_____

_____

_____

_____

_____

_____

_____

_____

Word Box

- enormous
- towering
- long
- sleepy
- grand
- content
- bright

Descriptive Language

Write a more descriptive word or phrase beside each one below.

1. walked home _____

2. shiny _____

3. yellow _____

4. she said _____

5. bird sang a song _____

6. one day _____

7. house on the corner _____

8. read to herself _____

9. blue _____

10. happy _____

11. tired _____

12. ate dinner quickly _____

Student Writing Sample: Christmas

I used to live in Idaho. On one snowy, December day on Christmas morning, I was awakened by my mom. She told me to get up and to get in my Christmas dress that had a tree, snowflakes, snowmen, and snow angels on it. It was a white dress. I put on my coat, boots, gloves, hat, and mufflers. It was cold when I went outside. I saw white stuff. What was it? Snow! We got in the snow-covered car. My mom, Tammra, and sister, Laura, were in the car, too. After a short drive, we arrived at my grandma's house. It is a brick red house with stairs to the front door. I was so happy when we got to my grandma's house. My aunts and uncles and three cousins were there before we got there. We ate lots of stuff. I can tell you one of them. The one is strawberry cream filling cake that we ate.

—Jaimee T.

Persuasive Voice

Objective

The student will read a text and determine whether the writer is sharing information or trying to persuade the reader.

Skills

- understanding the difference between telling and persuading
- identifying persuasive writing
- writing to persuade

Materials

—"Educating Kids Will Solve Many of Our Problems" (page 69)

—student copies of "Let Me Persuade You" (page 70)

—student copies of "Which Is It?" (page 71)

—student copies of "Persuasive Planning" (page 72)

—writing paper

—pencils

—"Student Writing Sample: Dear Mr. Lincoln" for teacher reference (page 73)

Procedure

1. Explain to the students that authors have different purposes when writing. The purpose might be to entertain or to convey information to the reader. Sometimes an author uses words to describe something.

2. Explain that authors sometimes use writing to try to persuade or convince the reader. The author has a strong opinion about something and wants the reader to feel the same way.

3. Discuss the different reasons an author might have for using persuasion in writing.

   - The author wants to change people's opinions.
   - The author wants people to get involved.
   - The author wants something to change.

4. Read aloud "Educating Kids Will Solve Many of Our Problems."

5. Discuss the article and ask the following questions:

   - To whom is the letter written?
   - What does the author think is the most important issue?
   - What does the author think education can do?
   - In what way is the author trying to persuade the president?
   - What does she want the president to do?
   - Do you agree or disagree with the author? Why?

Persuasive Voice *(cont.)*

6. Explain that the purpose of the letter is to change the president's mind and persuade him to make education a priority.

7. Distribute copies of "Let Me Persuade You" on page 70. Have each student complete the page by writing the points used by the author to convey her message.

8. Next, distribute student copies of "Which Is It?" on page 71. Each student completes the page by determining whether the sentence is telling or persuading.

9. After completing the page, discuss the ways the students determined which sentences were telling and which were persuading. What kinds of words were used in order to persuade?

10. Point out that when persuading, an author tries to tell the reader what he or she should do or believe. The author gives reasons why the reader should feel as the author does about the issue.

11. Distribute copies of "Persuasive Planning" on page 72. The student is asked to select a topic and plan a persuasive article.

12. Instruct each student to use "Persuasive Planning" to write an article, using carefully selected words to persuade the reader.

Publication

1. Have students work together to revise and edit their work.

2. Encourage students to read and discuss their articles with classmates.

3. Display the students' persuasive articles on a bulletin board entitled, "Are you Convinced?"

Extension

1. Post the students' persuasive articles in the hallway or visit other classrooms to share them. Invite the students to tell whether or not they were persuaded by the articles.

2. Have each student write a persuasive letter to a person of choice using a word-processing program. To make a professional letter, use a letter template. For Microsoft Word, click to open a new document. Then click on the *Letters and Faxes* tab. Select the type of letter template to be used—professional, contemporary, or elegant. Then click *OK*. The template will appear with text labeling the letter sections. Have the student type his or her name and return address, the recipient's name and address, and the body and closing of the letter. Any unnecessary sections of the template can be deleted. Be sure to have the student use the spell-check tool before printing the letter.

Educating Kids Will Solve Many of Our Problems

Dear Mr. President,

If you asked me what to do first, I would tell you to improve education. Education is the most important issue of all. Education can boost the economy, prevent homelessness, help stop the spread of AIDS, and help save the environment.

The president should spend more money on public schools. The money would help the schools buy much needed computers and Internet software. In California, schools are very crowded. To help this problem, more schools need to be built. More scholarships need to be available so students can have an opportunity to attend college.

Education is very important. If you have an education, you can obtain a job more easily than someone who doesn't. If you don't have an education, you probably won't earn a very good wage. You might become homeless or be on welfare. Having a good education could stop homelessness, boost the economy, and help people know the facts about AIDS. With this knowledge, a person can hopefully make the right choice to avoid getting AIDS. In this way, education may save many people from contracting the disease. The money saved could go into AIDS research.

Education can also help the environment. In schools, students will learn how important the environment is, and maybe they will work hard to save the earth from pollution. Students will be encouraged to recycle, reduce, and reuse, therefore making the world a better place.

Just by improving education, America can help prevent future homelessness and raise awareness of AIDS, maybe even prevent some people from contracting this extremely deadly disease. Education can also help show us how to save our earth.

Mr. President, by improving education you will help people have a better life in America.

Sincerely,

Maria Judnick, 11
Alex Anderson Elementary
San Jose, California

Let Me Persuade You

Use "Educating Kids Will Solve Many of Our Problems" (page 70) to complete this page.

1. What does the author think the president should do?

   _____

   _____

2. What are four things the author says will change with increased education?

   a. _____

   b. _____

   c. _____

   d. _____

3. Did the author make you think differently about this issue? Why?

   _____

   _____

   _____

4. Tell why you agree or do not agree with the author.

   _____

   _____

   _____

Which Is It?

Write *telling* or *persuading* beside each sentence. If the sentence is telling, rewrite it to make it persuasive.

_____   1. It's time that we all helped out to end air pollution.

_____

_____   2. If you have never been skiing, you're missing out on one of the best experiences you can have.

_____

_____   3. The dogs next door are always barking.

_____

_____   4. If we all pick up the litter on our streets, we can help our environment in many ways.

_____

_____   5. Rain forest land is destroyed every day.

_____

_____   6. Some people in our city arc homeless.

_____

_____   7. The cafeteria is so noisy.

_____

_____   8. If we had better books in the library, kids would read more.

_____

Persuasive Planning

Think of a strong opinion you have about an issue. Plan an article to persuade someone to share your opinion.

My topic: _____

My opinion: _____

Reasons I feel strongly about this opinion:

_____

_____

_____

_____

Facts that support my opinion:

_____

_____

_____

_____

Why other people should feel the same way:

_____

_____

_____

_____

Student Writing Sample:
Dear Mr. Lincoln

Dear Mr. Lincoln,

I really think you should be president. But my family thinks differently. My brothers think you are a sissy. My mother (please don't be offended) thinks you are kind of ugly. My father is the only other one who thinks you should be elected. I think a lot more women and young men would vote for you if you grew a beard. It would be quite helpful.

For example, the boys would think you were more manly with some hair on your chin. As for the women in my state, they think beards are quite handsome.

The majority of our state's votes would most likely go to you if you just wore a beard to the election next week. You could cut it off afterward if you didn't like it. Please, please grow a beard! It would help you a lot.

Sincerely,

An admiring girl from Pennsylvania

—*Cassondra Z.*

Descriptive Verbs

Objectives

The student will identify strong verbs in text. The student will select strong, descriptive words to use in writing.

Skills

- identifying descriptive verbs
- recognizing the purpose of descriptive verbs
- creating a list of descriptive verbs
- replacing flat verbs with descriptive verbs

Materials

—chart paper

—marker

—"Sweden's Igloo Inn" (page 76)

—old magazines (Check to be sure they are appropriate for students.)

—scissors

—glue

—construction paper

—student copies of "Using Descriptive Verbs" (page 77)

—student copies of "Strong Verbs" (page 78)

—student copies of "Using Strong Verbs" (page 79)

—"Student Writing Sample: My Blue Friend" for teacher reference (page 80)

Procedure

1. Explain to the students that when writing descriptively, we tend to focus on the use of adjectives, but verbs can be descriptive, too.

2. Write the sentences below on chart paper.
    - The animals <u>ran</u> in the forest.
    - The animals <u>frolicked</u> in the forest.

3. Point out to the students that the verb *ran* is acceptable to use, but the word *frolicked* is much more descriptive. It tells us that the animals were moving briskly and playfully through the forest.

4. Write the following list of verbs on chart paper and have the students brainstorm descriptive verbs that can replace them. (Suggested verbs are in parentheses.)
    - talk (*whisper, chat, mutter*)
    - yell (*shriek, scream, bellow*)
    - jump (*leap, hop, bound*)
    - eat (*gobble, nibble, taste*)
    - see (*peer, spy, witness*)
    - close (*latch, block, bolt*)
    - laugh (*giggle, snicker, chuckle*)

Descriptive Verbs *(cont.)*

5. Read aloud the article, "Sweden's Igloo Inn" on page 76.

6. As you read, have the students raise their hands when they hear descriptive verbs. Write these verbs on chart paper. Ask the following questions:

   • How do these verbs add to the story?

   • Were you able to create visual images of the story?

   • Which descriptive words were particularly memorable?

7. Explain that the author uses these verbs to give the reader a clearer visual image of what is happening in the story.

8. Next, distribute copies of magazines for the students. Instruct the students to look for advertisements with descriptive verbs.

9. As they find the verbs, the students cut them out and glue them onto construction paper. Have the students store the pages in their writing portfolios for future reference.

10. Distribute student copies of "Using Descriptive Verbs" on page 77. The students should complete the page by writing a series of descriptive verbs for each verb listed.

11. Ask each student to select a previously written story from his or her writing portfolio.

12. Instruct the student to underline all of the verbs used. The student should then replace each verb with a more descriptive verb.

Publication

1. Have the students recopy their stories with the newly added descriptive verbs. Instruct partners to revise and edit their work.

2. Invite students to read their first and second versions of their stories. Encourage classmates to respond to the changes made and the use of descriptive verbs.

3. Display student work on a board entitled, "Vivid Verbs."

Extension

1. Show the students how to find new verbs by using the thesaurus feature of a word-processing program. To use the feature in Microsoft Word, the student types a verb and then highlights it. Then the student clicks on *Tools* in the menu bar at the top of the screen and selects *Language . . . Thesaurus* from the drop-down menu. A window will appear, listing different word choices. The student can select a word from the window to replace the word that was originally highlighted.

2. Instruct students to read two or three articles from magazines or newspapers. The students will create a list of descriptive verbs found in the articles.

3. For added practice with using strong verbs, have the students complete "Strong Verbs" on page 78 and "Using Strong Verbs" on page 79.

Sweden's Igloo Inn

Sometimes on a very chilly night, the cold creeps in. It creeps beneath the thickest blankets, through the warmest pajamas, inside the coziest socks, until . . . Brrrr! It finds a set of toes to nip.

At the Ice Hotel in Jukkasjaervi (You-kus-yair-vee), Sweden, the cold doesn't have to sneak in. Guests who spend the night at the hotel expect the cold to nip at their toes. And their fingers. And their noses. That's because the entire hotel, from the floor to the ceiling to the walls and some of the furniture, is made of ice and snow!

Why would anyone spend money to stay in a snow fort? Kerstin Nilsson, a manager at the hotel, says its natural beauty attracts many guests. "It is pure winter: white and fresh snow, cold, beautiful northern lights in the sky and absolute quiet," she says. Guests who survive the 20 degree temperatures receive a printed Ice Hotel Certificate to prove they have conquered the cold. Says Nilsson: "After they spend the night, in the morning they feel like Tarzan or He-Man because they slept in there."

For eight years, a shiny new Ice Hotel has been built from fresh ice and snow each winter. Last year about 4,000 people checked in for a night at the Ice Hotel. Included in the $80 room charge are an extra warm snowsuit and a mummy-style sleeping bag. Guests need all the extra padding they can get: the hotel's 100 "beds" are actually ice blocks covered with reindeer skins! One hotel visitor, Kim Kovel of New York City, said she had started to have second thoughts about spending the night there. "It's freezing!" she said. "Apparently everybody makes out O.K. But after I saw the beds, I got a little worried."

By May, warmer temperatures will melt the hotel into a giant puddle. But it's not gone for good: builders will start chipping away at another Ice Hotel in October.

Using Descriptive Verbs

Write two or more descriptive verbs to replace each verb below.

1. shout _____

2. move _____

3. sleep _____

4. play _____

5. talk _____

6. work _____

7. make _____

8. drink _____

9. write _____

10. jump _____

Strong Verbs

Write a verb on each line. Use the words in the Word Bank to help you.

1. The squirrel _____ on the nut.

2. I wanted to surprise my mom, so I _____ into the room.

3. I got mad and _____ off.

4. When I _____ my dinner, my mom said to eat more slowly.

5. She _____ over her shoulder and saw the boy chasing her.

6. He _____ at the math problem for a long time.

7. My dad _____ back and forth because he was worried.

8. The girl _____ at the handsome movie star.

9. The hungry lion _____ his kill.

10. The people _____ slowly down the path.

11. The coach _____ at the players when they lost the game.

12. He _____ so no one heard him except his friend.

13. The girl _____, "I hurt my arm."

14. The lady _____, "I am so tired."

Word Bank

strolled	gobbled	whispered	tiptoed
nibbled	roared	glanced	paced
devoured	sighed	stared	stomped
cried	gazed		

Using Strong Verbs

Write a descriptive verb on each line. When you are finished, share your paragraph with a classmate.

The big, hungry lion _____ through the jungle. The hunter _____ up

as close as he could get to the lion, as he _____ his snack of trail mix. He hid

behind some bushes and _____ at the lion. His guide _____, "That

is the biggest lion I have ever seen!" The lion sniffed the air and turned and _____

at the hunter and his guide hiding in the bushes. Suddenly the lion flopped down on the jungle floor

and _____ the deer he had just killed. "Let's get out of here," _____

the hunter. "I don't like the way that guy eats!"

Student Writing Sample:
My Blue Friend

One ordinary day on Earth, I was walking down the street when all of the sudden somebody grabbed me. They put me in something that looked like a spaceship. I rubbed my eyes to see if I was dreaming. It was a spaceship! Was I being dragged into outer space? I got up, looking puzzled. If I was in a spaceship, where would I be going? Mars? The thought sent chills down my spine. I looked around the ship. All I could see were little knobs and buttons. Then I turned around and saw it—a real little blue Martian. When I turned, it was still there. I screamed in fright. Then I fainted to the floor.

The Martian said, "Who are you?"

"I'm Tana," I said with my voice trembling. "Who are you?" I said with my voice still trembling.

"I'm a blue Martian from the planet Mars."

"What are you going to do with me?"

"I'm going to experiment on you."

"What kind of experiment?"

"I'm going to take you to Mars to see if you can live."

"No, I can't live. I wouldn't be able to breathe."

"Then let's try and find out."

She opened the door to the ship and I stepped out. I couldn't believe it! I could breathe with no helmet or oxygen!

"See, you belong on Mars, so you'll stay here forever. Will you?"

"Yes, I will."

"That's great because it gets so lonely here. I wanted someone to play with."

"Why not pick one kid from Earth?"

"So, you promise you'll stay here and live with me?"

"Yes, I'll never leave."

So Tana and the blue Martian played forever.

—Tana S.

Using Adjectives in Writing

Objective

The student will identify adjectives in a text and use adjectives in written work.

Skills

- understanding the use of adjectives
- using adjectives in writing

Materials

—"Horsing Around" (page 82)

—chart paper

—markers

—student copies of "Practice with Adjectives" (page 83)

—student copies of "Senses" (page 84)

—"Student Writing Sample: Weather" for teacher reference (page 85)

Procedure

1. Review with the students the need for including descriptive language when writing.

2. Remind them that the use of descriptive words adds interest to a story and allows the reader to create mental images of what happens in the story.

3. Explain to the students that "Horsing Around" on page 82 uses descriptive language. Remind the students that adjectives are words that describe. Then ask the students to listen for adjectives as you read the story. Write these words on chart paper.

4. Invite the students to share about their abilities to picture the events of the story.

5. Next, display several sheets of chart paper. Label each with a different category, such as "Words Describing Sounds," "Words Describing Texture," "Words Describing Tastes," etc.

6. Keep the lists on display for use in future writing projects.

7. Ask each student to write his or her own story with adjectives.

Publication

Encourage each student to read aloud his or her story. Ask classmates to raise their hands each time they hear an adjective used in the story.

Extension

1. Instruct each student to make a list of adjectives describing objects in the home.

2. For additional practice, have students complete "Practice with Adjectives" on page 83 and "Senses" on page 84 for practice using senses to write descriptively.

Horsing Around

Today, at long last, I got to ride Uncle Jim's horse, Fancy, all by myself! Every time I visit Aunt Zoe and Uncle Jim, I head straight to the barn. I feed and brush Fancy. I fill my pockets with carrots and apples. When she carefully eats the treat from my hand, it gives me goose bumps. Her muzzle is so warm, and her big black eyes are beautiful.

Fancy is Uncle Jim's pride and joy. She has a coal black coat, mane, and tail. Aunt Zoe says Fancy is "spirited." That means she has lots of energy. And that is why she's not a good horse for a beginner. I have lots of energy, too, so I don't see the problem. Besides, I can tell Fancy likes me.

Anyway, Uncle Jim would saddle Fancy. Then he would set me up on her back as he led her around the pasture. While we walked, Uncle Jim would give me riding tips. He showed me how to hold the reins and what to do with my legs. He had done that three days in a row, and tomorrow I had to go home.

This morning I brushed Fancy as usual. Then I carried the saddle blanket for Uncle Jim. I watched as he saddled her. He picked me up and put me in the saddle, and we walked to the pasture. I held the reins while he gave me a look. "OK," he said. "I guess now's as good a time as any." And he let go.

I tried to remember what Uncle Jim had taught me. I was excited and nervous. I pressed the left rein across Fancy's neck, turning her head to the right. Then I put my heels to her ribs. She turned right and headed off just as I wanted! "This is the best moment of my life," I thought. Pretty soon I decided we should go faster. I pressed her ribs with my knees and clicked my tongue. Before I knew it, we were going fast along the fence. Cool! When we reached the end of the pasture, I turned Fancy around in a wide U. Her nose was pointed for the barn. That must have reminded her of dinner, because at that point she took off at a run. I was holding on for dear life and bouncing all over. "Whoa, Fancy?" I screeched. I pulled back the reins with all my might.

Fancy was headed for her stall, and I couldn't stop her. The barn door opening was coming up FAST, and it looked mighty small. I held my body close to Fancy's neck and buried my face in her mane as we raced into the barn. If she'd had brakes, they would have squealed as she slid into her stall. I turned around to a laughing Uncle Jim and said, "I'm ready to go again!"

Practice with Adjectives

Add adjectives to the sentences. Make them as interesting as possible.

1. The _____, _____ fire engine roared down the street.

2. The _____, _____ girl was scared.

3. The _____, _____ cat meowed softly.

4. The _____, _____ apple was good.

5. The _____, _____ bug walked across the floor.

6. The _____, _____ bird sat on the wire.

7. The _____, _____ star shone in the sky.

8. The _____, _____ clown made me laugh.

9. The _____, _____ flower smelled very good.

10. The _____, _____ chair was nice to sit it.

Senses

Read each word below. Use your senses to describe it.

1. **chocolate**

   looks: _____

   feels: _____

   smells: _____

   sounds: _____

   tastes: _____

2. **popsicle**

   looks: _____

   feels: _____

   smells: _____

   sounds: _____

   tastes: _____

3. **pizza**

   looks: _____

   feels: _____

   smells: _____

   sounds: _____

   tastes: _____

4. **cotton**

   looks: _____

   feels: _____

   smells: _____

   sounds: _____

   tastes: _____

Student Writing Sample: Weather

I like the rainbow.

The black clouds mean it will rain.

The rain makes the tree feel better.

The sun is steamy.

I don't like the sun because it's too hot.

I go to the pool because it's so hot.

The wind is cool.

The wind is fresh.

—Daisy R.

Similes

Objective

The student will use appropriate words to create similes.

Skills

- identifying similes
- understanding the use of similes
- recognizing the use of the words *like* and *as*
- completing similes
- writing similes

Materials

—chalkboard

—chalk

—"A Super Bowl for Kids!" (page 88)

—student copies of "Similes Using *As*" (page 89)

—student copies of "Similes Using *Like*" (page 90)

—"Student Writing Sample: My Favorite Dessert" for teacher reference (page 91)

Procedure

1. Write the following simile on the chalkboard:

   as quiet as a mouse

2. Explain to the students that this is a simile and that a simile is a comparison that is used to describe something. If a person moves quietly through the house and no one can hear him, we say that he is being as quiet as a mouse.

3. Write the following simile starters on the chalkboard, excluding the words in parentheses:

   - as hard as _____ (*a rock*)

   - as cold as _____ (*ice*)

   - as sly as _____ (*a fox*)

   - as happy as _____ (*a clam*)

   - as easy as _____ (*pie*)

   - as slow as _____ (*a snail*)

   - as dry as _____ (*a bone*)

   - as bright as _____ (*the sun*)

   - as light as _____ (*a feather*)

Similes *(cont.)*

4. Have the students complete each simile. (Possible completions are included in parentheses.)

5. Draw the students' attention to the word *as* in each simile. Explain that the word *like* is also used in similes, such as the following:
   - ran *like* the wind
   - sang *like* a bird
   - hopped *like* a frog
   - glowed *like* a lantern

6. Read the first two sentences of "A Super Bowl for Kids!" (below):

   Rain pours out of the Florida sky like a waterfall. Mike Boyle is as wet as a sponge.

7. Ask the students to identify the simile in each sentence ("pours like a waterfall," "wet as a sponge").

8. Draw the students' attention to the fact that similes provide readers with vivid descriptions and help to create visual images. For example, in the article, the rain was not coming down lightly. It was falling hard. Mike Boyle was not just a little bit wet. He was soaked.

9. Read aloud the remainder of the article.

10. Have each student write about a topic of interest, including at least one simile for description.

Publication

1. Instruct each student to illustrate one of the similes in "A Super Bowl for Kids!"

2. Have each student illustrate a simile that was used in his or her original story.

3. Display the students' written work on a bulletin board entitled, "As Good As It Gets!"

Extension

1. Make a simile game for students to play together. Duplicate the simile cards on pages 89 and 90 and cut them apart. (Laminate, if desired.) To play, a student selects a card, reads it to the class, and completes the simile.

2. Have student pairs work together to create different versions of the same simile. For example, the simile *as hard as a rock* can also become the following:
   - as hard as a stone
   - as hard as a brick
   - as hard as metal
   - as hard as concrete
   - as hard as nails

A Super Bowl for Kids!

Rain pours out of the Florida sky like a waterfall. Mike Boyle is as wet as a sponge. Mike plays quarterback and returns punts for the Huskies of Plymouth, New Hampshire. The Huskies are playing the Bandits of Port Charlotte, Florida, in a final game at the 1997 Pop Warner national championships.

Mike fields a punt and takes off. He splishes and splashes. He zigs and zags. Eighty yards later, he reaches the end zone. Touchdown!

"As soon as I broke into the open, I was thinking touchdown," says Mike, age 13. "I also thought, Don't mess up."

Mike's touchdown was the only score in the game. The Huskies won, 6–0. They were crowned a Pop Warner National Champion.

Mike is one of 300,000 kids, ages 5 to 16, who play Pop Warner football across the country. The kids compete in five divisions. Kids are divided by age and weight.

The Pop Warner national championships are held each December in Orlando, Florida. The event is called the Pop Warner Super Bowl.

The road to the Pop Warner Super Bowl is a long one. Teams begin training in early August. They play as many as 10 games during the season. Each team then must win its regional championship to advance to the Super Bowl.

Eric Frampton, 14, played right tight end for the Roughriders of Oak Grove, California. The Roughriders had won their division championship for the second year in a row.

"I really wanted to win again because this is my last year in Pop Warner," says Eric.

Cesar Vallejo, 12, played for the Mexicali (Mexico) Halcones [hal-CONE-ehs]. They were the first team from Mexico to play in the Super Bowl.

The Halcones lost their first game. The loss didn't bother Cesar.

"It meant a lot to our team to play in the U.S.," says Cesar. "It's something I will always remember."

Similes Using *As*

Laminate and cut apart the cards below. Take turns completing the similes.

as soft as _____	as quiet as _____	as strong as _____	as slow as _____
as sweet as _____	as big as _____	as hard as _____	as weak as _____
as quick as _____	as cute as _____	as tiny as _____	as sharp as _____
as gentle as _____	as loud as _____	as dark as _____	as scary as _____
as brave as _____	as fluffy as _____	as bright as _____	as cold as _____

Similes Using *Like*

Laminate and cup apart the cards below. Take turns completing the similes.

_____ like a waterfall	_____ like a turtle	_____ like a lion	_____ like thunder
_____ ike a firecracker	_____ like a tornado	_____ like the ocean	_____ like the desert
_____ like a building	_____ like a bird	_____ like a monkey	_____ like a mountain
_____ like ice cream	_____ like a haunted house	_____ like a giraffe	_____ like cotton
_____ like a leaf	_____ like a coyote	_____ like a tree	_____ like grass

Student Writing Sample:
My Favorite Dessert

My favorite dessert of all time is a puffball ice cream thing that you can get at a restaurant downtown. It is incredibly delicious! It is kind of like a crouton with ice cream and hot fudge inside of it. Yummy! It practically melts in your mouth! You also can get lots more food there that tastes like heaven. If I could have one thing to eat for every dessert, I would definitely pick this. That dessert makes my mouth water.

—Lindsey W.

Writing with Sounds

Objective

The student will use onomatopoeia in written work.

Skills

- understanding the use of onomatopoeia
- brainstorming words that represent sounds
- using onomatopoeia in writing

Materials

—chart paper

—marker

—"Will TV Violence Get Zapped?" (page 94)

—student copies of "Listen to This" (page 95)

—student copies of "What Do You Hear?" (page 96)

—student copies of "Listen" (page 97)

—writing paper

—pencils

—"Student Writing Sample: Noises" for teacher reference (page 98)

Procedure

1. Write the word *onomatopoeia* on the chalkboard. Pronounce the word for the students.

2. Explain that when writing, we can describe the sounds we hear. Words that sound like the sound themselves are called onomatopoeia.

3. Write the words below on chart paper and ask the students to tell the sounds made by each. (The sound is written in parentheses.)

   - bee (*buzz*)
   - cat (*meow*)
   - popcorn (*pop*)

4. Tell the students that the use of sound words adds interest to a story. Authors often use descriptive words to help readers create visual images. The use of onomatopoeia is similar to the use of adjectives, except the images are auditory rather than visual.

5. Write the sentences below on the chalkboard.

   - The noise of the fire kept us awake.
   - The crackling and popping of the fire kept us awake.

Writing with Sounds *(cont.)*

6. Ask the students to compare the two sentences.

    - Which one is more descriptive?
    - What makes one sentence more interesting than the other?
    - Does the second sentence help you to hear the sound of a fire?
    - What other words can be used to describe the sound a fire makes?

7. Explain that the use of the words *crackling* and *popping* creates sound images just like the use of adjectives creates visual images.

8. Explain that the article for this lesson contains one use of onomatopoeia. It uses the word *zap*.

9. Read "Will TV Violence Get Zapped?" aloud.

10. Distribute copies of "Listen to This" on page 95. The students complete the page by writing sound words for each of the items listed.

11. Have each student write a story including at least one example of onomatopoeia.

Publication

1. Encourage the students to share their stories with the class, using special sound effects for the sound words used.

2. Display the students' onomatopoeia stories on a bulletin board entitled, "Did You Hear That?"

Extension

1. Instruct the students to look through previously written stories in their writing portfolios. Have the students find appropriate places to add onomatopoeia in their stories.

2. Ask each student to write an onomatopoeia list of sounds made at home. Provide copies of "What Do You Hear?" on page 96 for categorizing words.

3. For added practice, complete "Listen" on page 97.

Will TV Violence Get Zapped?

It's Saturday morning, a few years from now. You plop on the couch, hit the remote control and—zap! there's a blank, blue screen where your favorite action cartoon should be.

Don't worry. TV will still exist in the future. But thanks to a new law, some shows you watch now may be blocked from your TV—by your parents! President Clinton signed a bill that includes a plan for keeping violence off kids' TVs.

The new law says TV makers must put a special computer chip, called the V (for violence) chip, in new TV sets. The chip would read a special rating code at the start of every TV show. Programs would be rated in much the same way movies are rated now. Parents would be able to program the chip to zap shows rated high for violence or other grown-up content. A blank screen would appear instead of the show.

Almost all TV producers are against the V chip. They say it is illegal for the government to interfere with what they put on TV because the Constitution guarantees everyone freedom of expression. Some broadcasters plan to fight the V-chip law in court.

Bosses at TV networks and some cable channels say they already protect kids by including "parental-discretion" warnings before shows that are for adult viewers. The networks also say they have cut out much of the violence in their programs. Many studies show that the most violence is on cable programs.

What kind of TV scenes are too violent for kids? Cops shooting at criminals? An evening news story about a real war? The Skipper whacking Gilligan with his hat? Wile E. Coyote running into a buzz saw? Some experts say all those scenes are too violent for kids. Others say none of them is a problem.

"I don't know exactly how you define violence," says Lynn McReynolds of the National Association of Broadcasters. The new law requires all TV broadcasters to agree on a rating system.

The goal of the V-chip law is to cut down on the amount of violence in society. Some experts think TV violence may make kids more likely to behave violently themselves.

But many others say factors besides TV make kids violent. "If the president wants to have a summit on violence, let's get all the manufacturers and sellers of handguns into Washington," says Don Ohlmeyer, a president at NBC.

The V-chip law causes other problems. You can't add the chip to the TV you have. Parents would have to buy a brand-new TV with a chip installed.

Also, kids may figure out how to change the chip's settings. "Kids will learn to program it as fast as their parents," former House Speaker Newt Gingrich said.

But Gingrich thinks there might be a more effective way to cut down on the violence kids see on television: "If they did two hours of homework every night, they'd be watching less television."

Listen to This

Write a sound word (onomatopoeia) beside each item below.

1. train _____

2. bird _____

3. dynamite _____

4. sneeze _____

5. dog _____

6. snake _____

7. car brakes _____

8. ball _____

9. drum _____

10. doorbell _____

11. fire _____

12. horn _____

What Do You Hear?

Listen to the sounds around you. How can you write them in words? On the chart below, write the sounds in your community.

Animal Sounds	
Vehicle Sounds	
People Sounds	
Weather Sounds	
Other Sounds	

Listen

Complete the story by adding onomatopoeia in the blanks.

The kids in my neighborhood decided to plant trees in the park. Things have never been the same.

Each morning you can hear the _____ of the flocks and the _____

of bees near the flowers. They're beautiful sounds. The _____ of the trees and

the _____ of rain on their leaves is music to my ears. Our park is filled with life.

Now, on Saturdays, kids cheer, "_____!" as they play sports. Children picnic with

their families and enjoy the outdoors, listening to peaceful sounds like _____

and _____. Everyone enjoys our new park.

Student Writing Sample: Noises

Yawn! I turned over and looked sleepily at my wall clock. Tick-tock-tick. The little hand was pointing to the nine and the big hand to the six. It was nine-thirty. I turned over to sleep again. "Wait a minute, 9:30!!!!" I hopped out of bed, nearly stepping on Fuzz-ball. Meow, hiss! "Whoops, sorry Fuzz."

I pulled on my slippers and walked toward the door. Unfortunately, I was still tired and was looking longingly at the bed. Bam! "Ouch! Whoa! When did they put that door there?" As I walked out the door, I accidentally stepped on the start button to my brothers model train. Buzzzzzz it went as it started up. Then, soon after, chuga, chuga, chuga choo-choo! I walked past the train, ears plugged. Once I got around the train and its tracks, I accidentally bumped into one of the large terra cotta vases my mom keeps as decorations on the floor. Bump, kaboom! I expected to hear a crash, but luckily, the vase just tipped over. I told myself to ask Dad to pick that up later. (It was too heavy for me.)

I thought I heard someone whisper "Shhhhhhhh, she's coming!" But when I didn't hear anything else, I guessed I probably hadn't. Just as I stepped into the living room, the light switched on and everyone I knew popped out from hiding spots. "Surprise!" Balloons flew into the air. My wonderful Aunt Helen walked forward with my first present. "Here you are, sweetheart! Hope you're having a very happy birthday," she said. I smiled. Her voice was the best sound I had heard all day.

—Kayla F.

Idioms

Objectives

The student will identify idioms. The student will determine the meaning of idioms and use them in writing.

Skills

- identifying idioms
- determining the figurative meanings of idioms
- using idioms in writing

Materials

—"Racing a Tornado!" (page 101)

—student copies of "Common Idioms" (page 102)

—chart paper

—marker

—student copies of "Idioms" (page 103)

—writing paper

—pencils

—copy of "Idiom Cards" (page 104)

—"Student Writing Sample: The Skateboard" for teacher reference (page 105)

Procedure

1. Explain to the students that figurative language can be used to add interest to writing.

2. Read "Racing a Tornado!" on page 101.

3. After reading, remind the students of the following sentence:

   We had made it by the skin of our teeth.

4. Ask the students the following questions:
   - Do teeth really have skin?
   - What does this sentence mean?

5. Explain to the students that this means that they barely made it without being hurt.

6. Provide the students with the list of "Common Idioms" on page 102. (You may want to have the students keep the list of idioms in their writing folders for future reference.)

7. Discuss the meanings of the idioms, asking the students to determine the meanings and how they can be used in sentences.

8. After discussing the meaning of each idiom, have some fun with this concept by asking each student to illustrate the literal meaning of an idiom. For example, "There was a fork in the road," can be illustrated by showing a dinner fork lying on the street.

Idioms *(cont.)*

9. Next, use the list of idioms to write a paragraph as a class on chart paper. See the example below.

   One day *I woke up on the wrong side of the bed*. I was *feeling under the weather* and it was *raining cats and dogs* outside. I had so much to do. I knew I had *bit off more than I could chew*. I told my mom she could *count on me* to do my chores. I knew I shouldn't complain, so *I zipped my lips* and *stepped on the gas*. When I finished my chores, I sat down *to take a load off my feet*. My mom said, "You deserve a nice treat for your hard work." *She read my mind*!

10. Provide the students with copies of "Idioms" on page 103. The students complete the page by writing the meaning of each idiom. Allow the students to work together, if necessary.

11. Ask each student to write a paragraph using at least three idioms.

Publication

1. Combine the students' literal illustrations of idioms (from step 8) into a class booklet. Display the booklet for all to enjoy.

2. Display the students' idiom paragraphs (step 11) on a bulletin board entitled "Figuratively Speaking." Invite the students to illustrate their paragraphs with literal or figurative illustrations.

Extension

1. Reinforce the use of idioms with a learning-center activity. Duplicate the idiom cards on page 104. Cut apart the cards and laminate them for durability. Place the cards in the learning center. To participate in the center, a student chooses an idiom card and illustrates it with the literal or figurative definition.

2. Encourage the students to create computer-generated illustrations of idioms by using a graphics program (such as *KidPix*) or a drawing program (in *Microsoft Word*).

3. Read a book of idioms to your students and have them identify the meanings of the idioms used. Here are two book suggestions:

   - *The King Who Rained* by Fred Gwynne
   - *Amelia Bedelia* by Peggy Parish

Racing a Tornado!

The Saturday Maria and I had picked for our 50-mile bike ride seemed perfect. We set out at 7 A.M. in beautiful spring weather. The air smelled fresh and clean. The sun shone brightly. Birds sang in the trees along the roadside. Wildflowers looked like flames of color waving in the fields. At 10:30 when we stopped for a break, we both felt terrific. As we rested, though, a brisk wind sprang up. That was when our perfect day began to change.

By noon, we knew a serious thunderstorm was blowing our way. A towering bank of dark clouds had rolled up out of the southwest. A stinging wind burned our faces. Stopping under a big oak tree, we frowned at each other with worry. There was no way to stay out of the storm. We would have to wait it out, but where?

Then things went from bad to worse. The temperature dropped suddenly. I looked up and saw that the sky now had a dark-greenish cast. Trees and crops were bent over by the wind. No animals were in sight.

Then a blue car pulled alongside our bikes. It was my aunt. She ordered, "Get in!" She looked frightened and we must have, too. We did as she said. That was when the hail started. Chunks of ice the size of golf balls pounded the windshield and dented the hood. Our tree would never have protected us, I thought, and silently thanked our rescuer.

My aunt sped northward with a determined look on her face. Could she outrun this storm? Maria and I looked backward at the black sky. That's when we saw it. Maria screamed. I yelled, "Tornado!" The funnel didn't look real, yet I knew it had to be. It was so close that I could see tree limbs, doors, and all sorts of other stuff that this monster had swallowed and was spinning around.

My heart had moved up to my throat and was beating so hard I thought it would leap from my body. I had never been so terrified. We would never outrun the tornado! It seemed to be moving closer. My aunt turned to us and said calmly, "We'll get through this. There's an overpass ahead. We'll pull in there for protection." She explained that we must lie flat in the lowest protected area.

Once we parked, we leapt from the car and lay pressed up against the concrete wall of the overpass. Not a minute too soon. Before I could count to twenty, a roaring surrounded us. It sounded like a freight train passing overhead. Then, suddenly, it was over. We had made it by the skin of our teeth.

Some trees were uprooted. Tree branches and flowers were scattered all over. Yet everything was calm and quiet.

We got to a phone and called home. Our parents had been worried sick. But soon we were all laughing with relief. We were shaken but excited. What a story I would have to tell at school!

Common Idioms

Store this list of idioms in a writing folder for future reference. Add others as you think of them.

a fork in the road

a frog in my throat

take a load off my feet

stopped dead in my tracks

a broken heart

bit off more than I could chew

swept off my feet

step on the gas

monkey around

changed my mind

costs an arm and a leg

got up on the wrong side of the bed

keep an eye on

stay in touch

read my mind

zip my lips

raining cats and dogs

feeling under the weather

count on me

Idioms

Write the meaning of each idiom below.

1. Take a load off your feet. _____

2. It broke my heart. _____

3. You're pulling my leg! _____

4. Keep an eye on your brother. _____

5. Zip your lips. _____

6. You can count on me. _____

7. It's raining cats and dogs. _____

8. I stopped dead in my tracks. _____

9. I could eat a horse. _____

10. I'm feeling under the weather. _____

11. Don't monkey around. _____

12. The toy costs an arm and a leg. _____

Idiom Cards

a frog in my throat	step on the gas
bit off more than he could chew	under the weather
got up on the wrong side of the bed	zip your lips
a fork in the road	raining cats and dogs

Student Writing Sample: The Skateboard

Ryan hopped out of bed and peered out the window. "Oh-man, it's raining cats and dogs outside!" Ryan said, to no one in particular. His brother, Tyler, walked groggily up beside him. "Sure is," he agreed. As he walked into the family room, his sister accidentally bumped into him. "Gosh! Watch where you're going!" she said as she stomped off. Tyler said, "Looks like someone got up on the wrong side of the bed."

Tyler walked off, leaving Ryan alone. He turned around when he heard a strange noise behind him. "Brent?" he called. His six-year-old brother jumped around and looked at Ryan with a very guilty look. "What were you doing?" Ryan asked. "Oh, nothing, nothing, not a thing!" He raced off. Ryan walked out to the kitchen. He looked at Brent, who was sitting at the kitchen counter and eating, then he whispered to his mom, "You might wanna keep an eye on Brent, Mom. He's acting kinda weird."

"All right, I'll keep my eyes peeled for trouble," she said.

After school, and after Ryan said hi to his mom and had a little snack, he went up to his room. When he got there, he saw Brent playing with Tyler's new skateboard. "You'll be seeing red if Tyler catches you playing with that," Ryan warned. Little Brent brought his hands up to his eyes. "I will?" he asked. "It means Tyler will be really mad," Ryan said. All of the sudden, Ryan was sandwiched between Brent racing out and Tyler racing in the room. "Ouch!" Ryan exclaimed as they all fell to the ground.

"Sorry," Tyler and Brent said at the same time. Then they rushed off to what they were doing. Ryan saw that Tyler had some wrapping paper in his hands. Suddenly Tyler turned to face Brent. "What were you doing in the room?" he asked, looking Brent straight in the eye. "Uh, er, well, I got a frog in my throat. Sorry!" he said and then raced off. Ryan thought he heard Brent mumble, "Red eyes," as he ran. Tyler looked confused for a moment, then shrugged his shoulders.

The next day Brent went straight up to Tyler and said, "Today's my birthday, remember?" "Of course I remember," Tyler said. Brent's eyes seemed to be searching Tyler for a present. Next, he tried Ryan. "Today's my . . . ," he started.

"I know, I know," Ryan said, holding out a freshly wrapped gift.

"Yeah!" he said, reaching out for the present.

"Not yet!" Ryan said, holding the present high above his head, then setting it on the table with some other presents.

The opening of presents was an uproar of ripping paper. But the last present was the best of all. "Here's a gift for the over-the-hill boy," Tyler said as he set a huge gift-wrapped box in front of Brent. "Wow, a skateboard! Thank you, Tyler!" he said as he gave Tyler a big hug. Though it was kind of corny, it was a good ending.

—Amber Q.

Writing with Rhythm

Objective

The student will create rhythm in writing by varying sentence length.

Skills

- understanding how varied sentence lengths create rhythm
- varying sentence lengths in writing

Materials

—chart paper

—marker

—"A Spooky Friend" (page 108)

—writing paper

—pencils

—student-appropriate magazines and newspapers (optional)

—student copies of "You've Got Rhythm" (page 109)

—"Student Writing Sample: Dear Ali" for teacher reference (page 110)

Procedure

1. Explain to the students that there are many elements to consider when writing a good story and capturing a reader's interest. One of these elements is the rhythm of the story.

2. Write the following sentences on chart paper:
   - Bats eat bugs.
   - They help farmers.
   - They feast on bugs.

3. Draw the students' attention to the fact that the sentences do not vary much in length. When the sentences are read aloud, there is a "boring" feel to the words. The words are visually similar in length and they have a similar number of syllables.

4. Next, write the following on chart paper:
   - Bats eat bugs.
   - They help farmers by feasting on insect pests that ruin crops.

5. Discuss the rhythm of these sentences. Draw the students' attention to the added interest and feel of the sentences. Explain that authors vary their sentence lengths in order to create emphasis and capture reader interest.

Writing with Rhythm *(cont.)*

6. Read aloud "A Spooky Friend" on page 108. As a class, count the syllables in each sentence of the first paragraph and record them on the chalkboard. (See below.)

   - *The sun slips below the horizon. (9 syllables)*
   - *A brisk wind blows leaves around your feet. (9 syllables)*
   - *Suddenly a vampire bat swoops down to suck your blood! (13 syllables)*

7. Ask the students if any of the sentences are the same length. Point out that two of the sentences are the same length, but the third sentence is longer and helps create rhythm by increasing the number of syllables. Why does the author vary the lengths of the sentences?

8. Continue to evaluate the number of syllables in the sentences of the remaining paragraphs.

9. Have each student select a simple topic about which to write. Instruct the student to write a paragraph about this topic.

10. Next, provide each student with a copy of "You've Got Rhythm" on page 109 to complete. The student selects a piece of writing (his or her own or from a magazine/newspaper) and evaluates the first five sentences. The student determines the sentence lengths and revises them as needed.

Publication

Have student pairs exchange stories to read and discuss, focusing on the use of varied sentence lengths. Ask partners to count the syllables in the sentences and then increase the sentence lengths when necessary.

Extension

1. Encourage students to word-process their paragraphs and then use the grammar check to ensure that sentences are not run-ons or fragments.

2. Provide students with articles from magazines and newspapers to evaluate for varied sentence lengths.

A Spooky Friend

The sun slips below the horizon. A brisk wind blows leaves around your feet. Suddenly a vampire bat swoops down to suck your blood!

OK, catch your breath. Scary stories about the many species of bats have been around for centuries. In real life, bats hardly ever hurt people. The furry, flying mammals are among nature's best environmentalists.

Bats eat bugs. They help farmers by feasting on insect pests that ruin crops. The 20 million Mexican free-tailed bats that roost near San Antonio, Texas, gobble up 250 tons of insects every night! Bats also snack on flies and mosquitoes that can get in your food or ruin a backyard barbecue.

Bats are also the Johnny Cactusseeds of the desert. They transfer pollen from cactus to cactus and spread the seeds around. Birds and other desert animals depend on cactus plants for food.

Actually bats, not people, should be afraid. Today 20 species of bats are on, or may soon be on, the endangered species list.

People who are afraid of bats have burned them out of caves or buried them inside mines or under city construction sites. "They think every bat is a vampire bat, and they kill all they can find," says Thomas Kunz, a Boston University biologist.

You've Got Rhythm

Read the text of a piece of writing. Evaluate the first five sentences of the text. Then write each of the sentences here, determining the number of syllables in each one. Finally, answer the questions and adjust the sentence lengths as needed.

Sentence #1: _____

Number of syllables: _____

Sentence #2: _____

Number of syllables: _____

Sentence #3: _____

Number of syllables: _____

Sentence #4: _____

Number of syllables: _____

Sentence #5: _____

Number of syllables: _____

Are the lengths of the sentences varied? _____

Do some sentences need to be revised? _____

Rewrite the five sentences below and read them to check for rhythm.

_____

_____

_____

_____

_____

_____

_____

_____

Student Writing Sample:
Dear Ali

Dear Ali,

    Today Lindsey S. is walking home from school with me. I live pretty close to the school, so it won't take too long. We are probably going to make a fort or something when we get home. Lindsey loves making forts with me. I like to make them, too. Then when we get it all finished, we will put a sign on it that says, "No Boys Allowed!" (The sign is for my brother.) Sometimes he gets mad at us!

                    Your friend,

                    Lindsey

                    —Lindsey W.

Writing with Alliteration

Objectives

The student will understand and use alliteration in writing.

Skills

- brainstorming words with the same initial letters
- creating alliterative sentences
- using alliteration in writing

Materials

—chart paper

—markers

—"Marathon Madness" (page 113)

—student copies of "Brainstorming for Alliteration" (page 114)

—student copies of "Alliterative Sentences" (page 115)

—writing paper

—pencils

—"Student Writing Sample: Siblings" for teacher reference (page 116)

Procedure

1. Review with your students the many ways to add interest to writing using descriptive tools.

2. Explain that alliteration is another tool that can be used. Define alliteration as the use of words that begin with the same letter.

3. Write the letter *S* on chart paper.

4. Ask the students to think of words (nouns, verbs, adjectives, adverbs, etc.) that begin with the letter *S*.

5. Show the students how the words can be used to make alliterative sentences, such as the following:

   - The silly snake slithered slowly on the sparkling sand.
   - Some sensational salamanders sang sweetly in September.
   - Six small snails slid slowly along the soppy sidewalk.
   - Seven sizable salmon swam in the sea.
   - Sometimes Sally sits by the school and sings.

6. Experiment with alliteration in the same manner using several different beginning letters.

7. Mention to the students that the title of the article for this lesson uses alliteration. The article is called "Marathon Madness." Ask the students to respond to this "catchy" title.

8. Proceed by reading the article to your students.

Writing with Alliteration *(cont.)*

9. Ask them to tell how alliteration might have been included in the article text to add interest.

10. Provide each student with a copy of "Brainstorming for Alliteration" on page 114.

11. The student completes the page by writing lists of words beginning with the same letters. This page can be stored in the student's writing folder for future reference when using alliteration.

12. For an added challenge, provide each student with a copy of "Alliterative Sentences" on page 115. The student reads a series of sentences and then uses words in the Word Bank to replace underlined words, creating alliterative sentences.

13. Next, instruct each student to select a topic of interest.

14. The student brainstorms a list of words beginning with the same letter as the topic.

15. Then the student writes a story or paragraph, incorporating alliteration into the writing.

Publication

1. Have each student create an illustration of alliterative sentences to post on a bulletin board display.

2. Encourage the students to read classmates' stories or paragraphs (step 12) and respond to the use of alliteration.

Extension

1. Write different letters of the alphabet on index cards and place them in a paper bag at a learning center. (Use letters such as *b, c, d, l, m, n, p, r, s,* and *t.*) A student randomly selects a letter card and makes a list of words beginning with that letter. The student then writes several sentences using words from his or her list.

2. Help your students find new words beginning with a particular beginning letter by showing them how to use the thesaurus feature of a word-processing program. For example, if a student wants to find a synonym for *walk* that begins with the letter s, the student types the word, highlights it, and then selects the thesaurus from the *Tools* menu (in *Microsoft Word*). A list of synonyms will appear. The student looks for a word beginning with s and then selects it to replace the typed word on the document.

Marathon Madness

What makes 15,000 men and women take off their jackets on a chilly day in April and run for four hours or more through the streets of Greater Boston? Put like that, it certainly sounds silly, but I was one of those runners. In fact, like everybody else, I even paid for the experience.

The race is called the Boston Marathon, and people have been competing in it since 1897.

"I could do that," I said.

"No, you couldn't," my friend Ed replied.

"Want to bet?" I said. And that's how it happened.

There were times when I regretted the dare. I had never run more than eight miles at a stretch before, and here I was training for over three times that distance. To make matters worse, since the race is in April, I had to run throughout the winter, and in Boston winters are cold. For most people just putting on their shirts, sweaters, jackets, mittens, and hats is exercise enough. I found myself out on the dark January streets, jumping over snow banks and skidding along icy patches of sidewalk. Even in gloves my fingers got so cold that they felt like rolls of pennies; my nose didn't defrost until lunchtime!

Finally, the big day arrived. The weather was cold with ice and rain.

Bang! A gun sounded, and we were off. Well, I didn't actually go anywhere at first because I was standing behind so many people I had to wait for them to move. It was like being in a traffic jam, so I just jumped up and down to stay warm.

At first, the running was easy. The other runners just seemed to pull me along. Somewhere around the 20-mile mark I even caught myself thinking, "This is nothing. Why did I train so hard?"

That's when I hit "the wall." I didn't actually run into a brick wall, but it felt as if I had. "The wall" is what marathoners call the point at which your body simply runs out of gas. My legs turned to rubber; my arms turned into pieces of wood. I thought I might pass out. I can't remember anything about the last five miles of the race.

I kept running though. At least, that's what Ed told me at the finish line.

"You looked good," he said. "How did it feel?"

"Terrific," I lied. I wasn't going to let him get the last laugh.

Brainstorming for Alliteration

Write a list of words beginning with each letter below.

T

_____

_____

_____

H

_____

_____

_____

W

_____

_____

_____

R

_____

_____

_____

C

_____

_____

_____

F

_____

_____

_____

On the back of this page, write sentences using many of the words in each list.

Alliterative Sentences

Create alliterative sentences. To do so, replace each underlined word with a word from the word bank that begins with the letter to the left. Recopy each sentence on the line below it.

c **words**   1. The cat sat on the pillow and meowed.

_____

_____

s **words**   2. One Saturday, a funny reptile moved in the dirt.

_____

_____

t **words**   3. Two little turtles walked to the city.

_____

_____

w **words**   4. The cold breeze blew past the lake.

_____

_____

p **words**   5. The rain sprinkled down on the street.

_____

_____

b **words**   6. The animal ate food for a meal.

_____

_____

Word Bank

wind	town	bear	pavement
silly	winter	tiny	whipped
pitter patter	poured	snake	slithered
berries	cushion	breakfast	sand
water	trotted	curled up	cried

Student Writing Sample: Siblings

"The sinister Sam slunk sneakily through the soft sand. Fortunately, he flopped and fell in the funky food. The end."

" That was a great story!" Nichole's younger siblings cheered.

"Thank you," said Nichole with a bow. The kids laughed. Suddenly Nichole rushed out the door. 12:00! It was 12:00. She ran as fast as she could to Lea's house. "Always late, you silly!" Lea said with a laugh.

Nichole blushed, then answered sheepishly, "Sorry, I was reading a book to the kids."

"Oh, excuses, excuses," Lea said, grinning. Nichole started to protest, but Lea said, "No matter. Let's start." Lea pulled a shiny blue handbag off her shoulder, and Nichole did the same (but hers was shiny purple). They then started trading. "Please pass the purple putty," said Lea.

"Like it?"

"Yes!" exclaimed Lea.

"What'll ya' give me?" asked Nichole.

"How 'bout this beautiful blue bird bracelet."

"O.K.," said Nichole.

After trading, Nichole headed home. As soon as she got home, the kids raided her room for treats. "Stop shaking out my new 'super sneaker' shoes, Stephen! Please put my pretty purple bag down, Pauleen!" On and on went the chaos, until Nichole finally said, "All right, all right. Here's the treat." She pulled out a lot of luscious lovely lollipops and let the kids grab. "Only one!" she said scoldingly as little Deven tried to grab two. He walked away, head down. Nichole grabbed her own pop and put the rest away as she lifted Deven onto her lap. "That's O.K., little buddy," she assured him. He hugged her. She smiled. Though they could be annoying, she had a great bunch of siblings.

—Brittney A.

Editing for Spelling

Objective

The student will edit for correct spelling.

Skills

- understanding the importance of correct spelling
- finding words in a dictionary
- identifying misspelled words
- correcting spelling errors

Materials

—"Rediscovering Jamestown" (page 119)

—chart paper

—marker

—dictionaries (one per student)

—student copies of "Before and After" (page 120)

—student copies of "Find the Errors" (page 121)

—student copies of "Spell Correctly" (page 122)

—"Student Writing Sample: *Jimmy Spoon and the Pony Express*" for teacher reference (page 123)

Procedure

1. Explain to your students how important it is to use correct spelling in writing. Using correct spelling helps another person easily read the student's work.

2. Read aloud "Rediscovering Jamestown" on page 119.

3. After reading the article, point out that some of the words are misspelled. Write the following sentence from the article on chart paper:

   Captain John Smith described the spot as "a verie fit place for the erecting of a great cittie."
   The students will notice that the words very and city are misspelled. This was not a mistake made by the author. The author was merely quoting what Captain John Smith had written.

4. Show the students how to identify a spelling error by writing *sp* above a misspelled word. Remind the students that a dictionary is a useful resource for spelling words correctly. Explain that not only is it important to identify words that might be misspelled but also the correct spellings need to be found.

5. Have the students practice using dictionaries. Distribute dictionaries and copies of "Before and After." Each student completes the page by looking up a word in the dictionary and then writing the words that come before and after it on the page.

6. Continue practice by providing each student with a copy of "Find the Errors" on page 121. On this page, the students read an article and try to identify the misspelled words.

Editing for Spelling *(cont.)*

7. After finding the words, each student completes "Spell Correctly," which allows the student to find the correct spellings of the words on the previous page.

8. Finally, instruct each student to write a story about a topic of interest.

9. Encourage the student to use difficult words related to the topic. A student should write a question mark above any words that he or she needs to check in the dictionary.

Publication

Divide the students into pairs and have them edit each other's letters. Encourage the students to use their dictionaries to check word spelling.

Extension

1. Have the students type their completed stories using a word-processing program. Show them how to use the spell-checking feature (usually found in the *Tools* menu). Explain to the students that when the spell checker identifies a misspelled word, it may provide a long list of suggestions for replacement. It is important to review carefully the list before selecting the correct spelling of a word. When the correct spelling is identified, the student highlights the word and clicks *okay* to change it on the document.

2. For additional practice with finding words in the dictionary, you may want to take a step back and have your students practice alphabetizing words that begin with the same letter. This will make it easier to find words in the dictionary. On the chalkboard, write three words that begin with the same letter, such as *blend*, *bat*, and *beg*. Draw the students' attention to the first letter of each word and remind them that, since they begin with the same letter, we have to look at the second letter. Underline the second letter of each word and have the students place the words in alphabetical order.

Rediscovering Jamestown

Brent Smith, 8, of Houston, Texas, cannot take his eyes off the skeleton. Lying in a glass case at the National Geographic Society in Washington, DC, the skeleton—with a bullet in its right leg—is a mystery. "I just need to know what happened to this guy," says Brent. "What was his name? How did he die?"

That's what historians are wondering, too. The skeleton is nearly 400 years old. It was found in Jamestown, Virginia, site of the first English settlement in America.

On May 13, 1607, a ship carrying 104 men and boys from England arrived at a peninsula in Virginia. The soil and climate seemed just right for a new home. Using old-fashioned spelling, Captain John Smith described the spot as "a verie fit place for the erecting of a great cittie." They named their settlement Jamestown.

The colonists built a triangle-shaped fort along the river to protect themselves from the Spanish and Native Americans. Over the next few years, disease, starvation, and attacks by the Powhatan tribe killed many settlers. In 1608, a fire ravaged the fort.

Eventually, Jamestown, Virginia's capital, shifted east of the original site. Then the governor of Virginia decided to move the capitol to nearby Williamsburg. Old Jamestown began to disappear—at least above ground.

But what about underground? During the 1940s and 1950s, archaeologists began to explore parts of Jamestown. They found many artifacts but believed that everything else must have washed away.

Archaeologist Bill Kelso didn't think so. In April 1994, he and others began digging at a tempting new spot: "There was a piece of ground, shaped like a triangle, that no one had ever put a shovel into."

His hunch paid off. Kelso and his team soon found bits of pottery that could only have been from the 1607 fort. "That first day, we knew we had found it!"

Since then, archaeologists have uncovered more than 180,000 artifacts from the early 1600s, including beads, keys, and toys. And only a fraction of the fort's grounds have been explored!

The recent discoveries are giving scientists and historians the best picture ever of how early colonists lived and died. "Archaeology is like a time machine," says Kelso.

Some of the most intriguing finds are skeletons of the first settlers. Anthropologist Doug Owsley of the Smithsonian Institute is thrilled to study these remains: "Bones tell you stories of what life was like for those people, what killed them, even what they ate."

So what about the skeleton on display in Washington? Who shot him? And why? Archaeologists hope to have more answers for kids like Brent Smith, who looks one last time at the skeleton and says, "Wow! I really like knowing what happened 400 years ago."

Before and After

Look up each word in the dictionary. On the lines, write the words that come before and after it on the dictionary page.

1. _____ reason _____

2. _____ system _____

3. _____ enormous _____

4. _____ provide _____

5. _____ atmosphere _____

6. _____ vertical _____

7. _____ substance _____

8. _____ announce _____

9. _____ crocodile _____

10. _____ measure _____

11. _____ examine _____

12. _____ damage _____

13. _____ society _____

14. _____ argument _____

Find the Errors

Read the article below. Underline the words you think are misspelled. Hint: There are at least ten misspellings.

A half-moon glowed in the night as a sleak white rocket blasted off from Cape Canaveral, Florida. A small spacecraft called the *Luner Prospector* was tucked in the rocket's nose. Soon *Prospector* broke free from the rocket and began to coast toward the shining moon.

For the first time since 1972, the U.S. space agensy NASA launched a mission to the moon in January 1998. If all goes well, *Prospector*, which carries no astornauts, will spend one year orbiting the moon. It will map the deeply cratered surrface. It will find out what the moon is made of and investigate the exciting chance that there is water there.

Says program scientist Joseph Boyce, who worked on NASA's 1972 moon trip: "It feels good to be going back."

Though *Prospector* won't land on the moon, scientists compare its mission to *Pathfinder's* thrilling trip to Mars. Both ships were built under NASA's new guidlines: "faster, cheaper, better." The missions are, says Boyce, "the start of the next golden age of ecsploration.

Prospector is less than half the weight of an average car. The spacecraft carries no computer or camera. But it is well equipped for its mission. Five instruments on its arms and antena will put together the most complete picture ever of the moon.

Eventully, *Prospector* will crash-land on the lunar surface. By then, scientists should know a lot more about the moon.

Some astronamers believe that the moon holds as much as a billion tons of ice left long ago by crashing commets. Commets are mixtures of dust and ice. Most of the ice would have melted, but some may be trapped in areas where the sun doesn't shine.

Ice on the moon could provide water so that astronuats, and maybe ordinary citisens, could live on the moon someday. An air supply would also be needed. But with the right equipment, people can live in strange places. "We have a year-round base in Antarctica," says Boyce. "Today's kids may end up living on the moon."

Spell Correctly

The words below were misspelled in the article on page 121. Look up the words in the dictionary to find the correct spelling. Write the correct spellings on the lines.

1. sleak _____

2. luner _____

3. agensy _____

4. astornauts _____

5. surrface _____

6. guidlines _____

7. ecsploration _____

8. waight _____

9. antena _____

10. eventully _____

11. astronamers _____

12. commets _____

13. citisens _____

Student Writing Sample:
Jimmy Spoon and the Pony Express

The main character in this story is Jimmy Spoon. He knows Shoshoni Indians because he lived with them. He also joined the Pony Express because he is a good horse rider. Nahanee is an Indian that Jimmy knows. Pen is Jimmy's friend, and he helps Jimmy a lot.

The setting takes place in a desert. This was a long time ago. The weather was hot. The terrain was rocky. Town was boring to Jimmy. Jimmy left Salt Lake City to begin his adventure.

The problem in the story is that Paiutes are attacking places. They char Ruby Valley Station. They attack Mr. Lantern, the stagecoach driver. They steal horses. It makes Jimmy angry.

The resolution is that Jimmy hides with the Shoshoni Indians. Jimmy visits Old Mother, Jimmy's friend. Pen comes with Jimmy. Jimmy stays longer. Jimmy decides to marry Nahanee.

My favorite part is when Jimmy is with the Shoshoni. He does a lot of interesting things there, such as riding horses. He goes to a Thanksgiving festival. At the festival they pray.

I would recommend this book because it's full of adventure.

—Nicholas W.

Using Paragraphs

Objectives

The student will write a paragraph using a main idea sentence and additional sentences to support the main idea.

Skills

- understanding the parts of a paragraph
- writing a paragraph with main-idea and supporting sentences

Materials

—chart paper

—marker

—"Back to the Moon!" (page 125)

—student copies of "Paragraph Practice" (page 126)

—student copies of "Dissect a Paragraph" (page 127)

—magazine or newspaper articles

—"Student Writing Sample: My Scary Story" for teacher reference (page 128)

Procedure

1. Explain to the students that good paragraphs begin with a main idea sentence.

2. Read aloud the first paragraph of "Back to the Moon!" on page 125.

3. Draw the students' attention to the fact that the first sentence tells the main idea of the rest of the paragraph. Continue the discussion by explaining that the other sentences in a paragraph are all used to support the main idea sentence.

4. Distribute copies of "Paragraph Practice" on page 126. The students complete the page by identifying the main idea and supporting sentences.

5. Read the remainder of the article aloud to students. Pause periodically to dissect a selected paragraph, identifying the main idea and supporting sentences.

6. Distribute copies of "Dissect a Paragraph" on page 127. Instruct each student to select an article and choose three paragraphs in the article to dissect. The student writes the main-idea sentence and two or three supporting sentences of each paragraph.

Publication

Instruct each student to write a paragraph about a selected topic. Have the students work together to check each other's paragraphs for the appropriate use of sentences.

Extension

Have each student select a previously written story from his or her writing portfolio. The student should check the paragraphs in the story, looking for the use of main-idea sentences.

Back to the Moon!

A half-moon was shining as the rocket's engines began to roar. People on the ground cheered as it blasted off from Cape Canaveral, Florida. "We're on our way!" said scientist Scott Hubbard.

A small spacecraft called *Lunar Prospector* was tucked inside the rocket's nose. An hour after takeoff, the spacecraft broke free again and began a 4 1/2-day trip to the moon.

The last time the U.S. space agency NASA sent a mission to the moon was in 1972. "It certainly feels good to be going back," said scientist Joseph Boyce.

There are no astronauts on board *Prospector*. It will not land on the moon. *Prospector* will spend a year traveling around the moon, studying it.

Prospector will help answer questions about the moon. How did the moon form? What is it made of? Could humans live there someday?

In 1963, NASA created the Apollo space program to explore the moon. The most exciting moment came in 1969 when astronauts landed on the moon. They did experiments and collected rocks. But Apollo left many questions unanswered.

Prospector has tools to map the moon's entire surface. Other instruments will study what type of minerals make up the moon. "Don't expect to see penguins skating around a lake!" says Boyce. But a water supply on the moon could make it possible for people to live there.

An air supply would also be needed. But with the right equipment, people can live in strange places. "We have a year-round base in Antarctica," says Boyce. "Today's kids may end up living on the moon."

Paragraph Practice

Read each paragraph. Underline the main idea in red. Underline the supporting sentences in blue.

Unlike silkworms, spiders cannot be raised on farms. So scientists are inventing ways of making spider silk without spiders. The ability to spin a web is controlled by certain genes inside the cells of spiders. Researchers at Monsanto and DuPont chemical companies have made copies of these genes and put them into certain easy-to-grow bacteria. The scientists' goal: bacteria that can churn out spider silk.

Finding new planets is no easy job. Even the biggest planets are small compared with stars, and they do not burn brightly. To find them, astronomers must look carefully at stars and watch for telltale wobbling patterns. From the patterns they can calculate whether a large planet-like object is orbiting the star and pulling on it with its gravity.

Many people have never heard of Nubia. Researchers have tended to ignore this ancient African land and focus instead on its neighbor to the north, Egypt. But today more archaeologists than ever are turning their attention to ancient Nubia, the world's first known black civilization.

Dissect a Paragraph

Locate an article to read. Dissect three paragraphs in the article. Write the main-idea sentence and two or three supporting sentences from each paragraph you chose.

Paragraph 1

Main idea: _____

Supporting sentences: _____

_____

_____

_____

Paragraph 2

Main idea: _____

Supporting sentences: _____

_____

_____

_____

Paragraph 3

Main idea: _____

Supporting sentences:

_____

_____

_____

Student Writing Sample:
My Scary Story

Once upon a time, there were four little girls. Their names were Rachel, Demeisha, Linda, and Sarah. They were teenagers. They went to a Halloween party and started dancing, playing, and singing. Well, just one of them was brave enough to go upstairs. Her name was Linda. She had to go to the bathroom to finish her makeup.

When she was in the bathroom, she saw a clown in the mirror and he said, "Boo!" She screamed. All the lights went off and her friends went to see what happened.

The girls were very scared. They tried leaving, but the door closed quickly. They heard someone say, "Ooooooo."

Sarah yelled, "Oh my gosh!"

Rachel replied, "Let's go home."

They were all walking home when, "Boo!" They were all frightened again.

—Rachel M.

Editing for Punctuation

Objectives

The student will recognize the importance of sentences using different types of punctuation. The student will edit written work for correct punctuation.

Skills

- recognizing the use of exclamatory and interrogatory sentences
- editing for the use of question marks and exclamation marks

Materials

—chart paper

—marker

—"No Helmet? Pay Up!" (page 131)

—student copies of "Something's Missing" (page 132)

—writing paper

—pencils

—"Student Writing Sample: The Best Thing That Ever Happened to Me" for teacher reference (page 133)

Procedure

1. Discuss with your students the importance of proper punctuation. (They will most likely understand that a punctuation mark of some kind is needed at the end of every sentence.)

2. Continue the discussion by explaining that varied punctuation in a story helps to add interest. Most of the time when we write we end every sentence with a period, but using questions and exclamations heightens interest, as long as they are not overused.

3. Write the following paragraph on chart paper.

    One day, Katie was walking home from school. She saw something sparkling in the grass. She was curious to know what it was, so she walked closer. There in the grass was a shiny, gold coin. She didn't know how it got there.

4. Next, write a revised version of the same paragraph on chart paper. (See below.)

    One day, Katie was walking home from school. She saw something sparkling in the grass. What was it? She was curious, so she walked closer. There in the grass was a shiny gold, coin! How did it get there?

5. Point out to the students that the story stayed the same, but the use of different types of sentences and punctuation helped to add interest.

6. Write the following paragraph on chart paper:

    The new trees do more than add color to the neighborhood. They are also part of a plan hatched by Comb's class to attract birds to the area. Birds are an "indicator species," which means that when they are living in an area, other animals are sure to follow.

Editing for Punctuation *(cont.)*

7. Have the students think of exclamatory or interrogatory sentences that can be added to the paragraph (or changed in the existing text) to add further interest and variation.

8. Read "No Helmet? Pay Up!" and emphasize the questions and exclamatory sentences used.

9. Explain that the author could have used only statements ending with periods, but that the use of different types of sentences makes the article more interesting.

10. Tell the students that they will complete a worksheet, looking for missing punctuation. Show them how to indicate the location of a needed punctuation mark by writing an editing "carrot" and then the punctuation mark. A carrot looks like this: ^

11. Distribute copies of "Something's Missing" on page 132. The students complete the page by using editing marks to add punctuation to the story.

Publication

1. Ask each student to select a previously written story from his or her writing portfolio.

2. Instruct the student to read the story and decide where questions and exclamatory sentences can be added to make the story more interesting.

Extension

1. Have each student select an article or a story to read. Instruct the student to locate different ending punctuation marks and note how these sentences create interest.

2. Divide students into pairs and have them write short scripts to perform for the class. In the scripts, the students include questions and exclamations and then emphasize these through expression and voice intonation when performing for the class.

No Helmet? Pay Up!

"Stop, kid! Get off that bike!" Kids in Florida who ride a bicycle without wearing a helmet risk hearing those words from the police. They might even have to pay $17 for breaking the law!

Florida has joined dozens of other cities and states across the country by passing a helmet law. In Florida the law applies to all kids under 16. With most helmet laws, kids who've received tickets don't have to pay the fine if they can prove that they later went out and bought a helmet.

Why are some states getting so tough on helmetless riders? Think of the last time you fell off your bike. Did you bruise your knee or scrape your elbow? Did you hit your head? Thousands of kids tumble off bicycles every year, and many suffer serious head injuries. Unlike a bruise or a scrape, a head injury can cause permanent damage. A very serious head injury can kill you. But helmets help. According to the National Safe Kids Campaign, bike helmets lower the risk of head injury 85%.

Simon Crider, 11, knows how important a helmet can be. In 1995 he was biking in Gainsville, Florida, when he hit a rock and flew over his handlebars. His head hit the pavement, and his helmet cracked. Luckily, it was his helmet and not his head that got damaged.

Still a lot of kids are not crazy about wearing helmets. Says Mighk (Mike) Wilson, a bicycle-safety leader in Florida: "A big part of it is the 'dork' factor. Some kids just don't think helmets are cool."

Not Simon. He thinks his helmet is plenty cool. "A helmet saved my life," he says. "Sometimes they mess up your hair, but it's worth it."

Something's Missing

Use editing marks to add punctuation where it is needed.

Save Our Streams

    Have you ever been boating on a river   You would expect to see clear water fish birds and healthy plants   Let me tell you about my trip down our local river

    I saw a refrigerator a dead cow and soda pop cans   I saw plastic cups sewer pipes and dirty water   I didnt enjoy this trip   There was too much pollution in the river

    I feel the president should make cleaning up our waterways one of the first things he does He should do this because we drink water from this river and other rivers like it   We need water We need it to be clean   We can get sick from dirty water and die

    I would like to see our rivers cleaned up   This would give us clean drinking water and a great place to fish   This could be done by removing the trash and waste products   Then we would make sure that they do not get put back into the river   Maybe our laws could be more strict People would think before they polluted our rivers

    When I grow up, I want to bring my son down the river   I want him to see only fish birds clean water and green plants   Wouldnt it be nice if he could also take a drink

---

Student Writing Sample: The Best Thing That Ever Happened to Me

The best thing that has ever happened to me was when I got to go to the beach. It was so fun! I got to go boogie boarding and make sand castles. When we go to the beach, we bring soda, licorice, and some chairs. But most of the time, we just bring chairs and tables. Sometimes the water is cold, but you get used to it. Have you ever been to the beach? Well, if you haven't, I'll tell you it's fun, and I want to go again!

—*Jenny H.*

Capitalizing Properly

Objectives

The student will use appropriate capitalization in writing.

Skills

- recognizing the need for capital letters
- editing for proper use of capital letters
- using editing marks to indicate capitalization
- capitalizing the names of months, places, names, etc.

Materials

—"A New Deal for Northern Ireland" (page 136)

—markers or colored pencils

—student copies of "A New Deal for Northern Ireland" (page 136)

—student copies of "Categorizing Capitals" (page 137)

—student copies of "Editing for Capitalization" (page 138)

—"Student Writing Sample: *Felicity Saves the Day* by Valerie Tripp" for teacher reference (page 139)

Procedure

1. Your student will surely understand the following uses of capitalization:

   - beginning of a sentence
   - names of people and places
   - the letter I

2. Explain that in this lesson, they will be identifying other categories of words that should be capitalized, such as the following:

   - names of countries/cities
   - names of months
   - a person's title (*President, Senator, Principal, Mrs., Dr., Mr.,* etc.)

3. Distribute copies of "A New Deal for Northern Ireland" on page 136.

4. Read the article together as a class.

5. Instruct the students to use a marker or a colored pencil to underline each of the capitalized words.

6. Discuss the words underlined by the students. Ask them to tell why the words are capitalized.

7. Then distribute copies of "Categorizing Capitals" on page 137. To complete the page, each student writes the capitalized words from the article under the appropriate category headings.

Capitalizing Properly *(cont.)*

8. Next, distribute student copies of "Editing for Capitalization" on page 138. To complete the page, each student reads the article and identifies words that need to be capitalized.

9. Before the students complete this page, explain that when editing, there are special marks to use when indicating letters that need to be capitalized. To indicate the need for a capital letter, the lowercase letter is underlined three times. Explain that when completing "Editing for Capitalization," each time a word is found, the student underlines the initial letter three times.

10. Have each student write a story that happened at a particular place. Instruct the students to use at least three different categories of capitalization, for example the names of places, the names of people, and the months of the year.

Publication

1. Divide students into pairs and have them edit each other's stories for proper capitalization. Remind the students to underline a lowercase letter three times to indicate the need for capitalization.

2. Show your students how the computer can assist in identifying words that need to be capitalized. Set *Preferences* on your word-processing program for *spell checking* as you type. To do this with *Microsoft Word*, select *Preferences* from the Tools menu. Click on the *Spelling & Grammar* tab and then check the box beside *Check Spelling as You Type*. Then have students type their stories. Misspelled words and words that need to be capitalized will be underlined in red. Students can make the necessary changes and the red lines will disappear.

Extension

Have the students locate and read newspaper articles, looking for the types of words that are capitalized.

A New Deal for Northern Ireland

Laura Lesley remembers the day the war hit closest to home. It was October 7, 1996. A bomb exploded near her school's playground in Lisburn, Northern Ireland. The attack was a sign that the latest attempt to bring peace to her country had failed.

"It was frightening. I'd never been close to a bomb before," said Laura, now 13. "I thought the school might get bombed next."

Violence has divided Northern Ireland for years. Towns are split into sections. Painted lines, brick walls, and barbed wire separate people of Protestant religions from their Irish Catholic enemies.

The Protestants, who make up most of the population, are mostly loyal to the British, who rule Northern Ireland. The Catholics mostly favor rejoining the rest of Ireland. They want to be one country, free of British rule.

Since 1968, nearly 3,300 people have died because of the fighting.

Leaders from the groups at war finally agreed that peace was what they needed. On April 10, 1998, they announced a historic plan to govern Northern Ireland together. The people of Ireland and Northern Ireland voted on the agreement on May 22, 1998.

"This agreement is a fair one," said former U.S. Senator George Mitchell. "It allows both communities to live together in peace." President Clinton sent Mitchell to Northern Ireland to help with the peace talks. His job was to bring the groups together.

England started trying to take over Ireland back in the 1100s. By 1651, England's King had claimed the land. Britain gave up rule of the Irish Republic in the south in 1921. But it would not give up Northern Ireland. Most Catholics in the north refused to accept British rule. Catholics and Protestants have been enemies ever since.

Under the agreement, a new 108-member group of Protestants and Catholics would begin to share decision making for the region. Also, the Irish Republic and Northern Ireland would begin to work together.

After her own close call with violence, Laura Lesley hopes the people of her country will live in peace.

Categorizing Capitals

Write each word below under the appropriate category heading.

Lisburn	April	England
Northern Ireland	U.S. Senator	Britain
October	Protestant	Clinton
Laura Lesley	George Mitchell	Irish Republic
Catholics	President	

Names of Months	
Names of Countries/Cities	
A Person's Title	
Names of People	
Names of Religions	

Editing for Capitalization

Locate the letters that should be capitalized but are not. Underline these letters three times each.

Keiko's journey began in the frosty blue waters of the atlantic ocean near iceland, where he was born about 20 years ago. At age 2, he was captured and taken to an aquarium in iceland. He would never swim with his pod again.

Soon after that, he was moved to an aquarium in canada and began performing tricks for people. But he didn't make his big splash until an aquarium in mexico bought him. That's where he landed the lead whale role in *free willy*. The hit movie made keiko a hollywood heavyweight.

In the movie, keiko's character suffers through awful living conditions in a theme park. In real life, keiko's situation wasn't much better. His pool at the aquarium in mexico was too small and too warm. His skin, once glossy and slick, broke out in sores. And the big fin on his back, called a dorsal fin, flopped sadly over to one side.

Keiko's fans rushed to his rescue. A group called the free willy keiko foundation raised enough money to fly him from mexico to a specially built pool in newport, oregon, in 1996. In his cool new pool, keiko's health improved right away. His skin sores disappeared, and he gained 2,000 pounds. Soon he was strong enough for a journey home.

While keiko was getting stronger, his caretakers were busy designing a new home for him in iceland. Because keiko had lived almost his whole life in captivity, it was too risky just to set him free. The solution was to build a giant floating pen in the north atlantic ocean. The pen is 250 feet long and has walls made of special nets so that fish swim in and out. Keiko can see and hear nearby whales and birds.

Student Writing Sample:
Felicity Saves the Day
by Valerie Tripp

There are three main characters in this book. Felicity is very smart and also likes to horseback ride. Penny, who is a horse, gets ridden every day. Grandfather always knows what's best. He also knows a lot of things. Everyone lives at Kings Creek Plantation. It is a big place.

This story takes place at Kings Creek Plantation and the woods. Grandfather owns Kings Creek Plantation. The plantation is wide in the yard and on the inside. The woods are a lonely place. No one sees any animals in the woods.

The problem in this story is that Ben runs away and stays in the woods. He has no food or water. Two men are coming to get him because he ran away from home. Ben doesn't know that two men are coming to get him. His father sent the two men. What is Ben going to do?

The resolution to this book is that Felicity comes to save Ben. Felicity rides Penny to the woods to bring food and water to Ben. Felicity tells Ben that two men are coming to get him. Felicity brings Ben back home. They tell the truth. Now everybody is happy, while Felicity rides along the road path.

My favorite part of this book is when Felicity finds her horse, Penny. Felicity lost her horse before, but Grandfather finds her. Felicity recognizes her horse.

I recommend this book to others because it's very detailed and it's realistic.

—Jordyn A.

Editing for Simple and Complex Sentences

Objective

The student will vary sentence length in writing.

Skills

- understanding the difference between simple and complex sentences
- identifying simple and complex sentences
- editing for the use of both simple and complex sentences

Materials

—"Creature Comforter" (page 142)

—chart paper

—marker

—student copies of "Simple or Complex?" (page 143)

—student copies of "Change It!" (page 144)

—writing paper

—pencils

—"Student Writing Sample: The Magic of Christmas" for teacher reference (page 145)

Procedure

1. It is important for your students to understand that sentence length makes a difference in the way an article flows. Explain that a smooth article has some simple sentences and some complex sentences.

2. Read aloud "Creature Comforter" on page 142. Discuss the flow of the sentences.

3. Define a simple sentence as one that has one independent clause. This means that it has one complete thought. See the example below.

   She wanted to take care of animals.

4. Next, define a complex sentence as one that has an independent clause and at least one dependent clause. This means that one or more parts of the sentence depends on another. See the example below.

   When Shanin Leeming was in second grade, she asked for a job.

5. Point out to the students that the independent clause is as follows: *she asked for a job*. This part of the sentence can stand on its own. The first part of the sentence is the dependent clause: *When Shanin Leeming was in second grade . . . .* This part of the sentence cannot stand on its own. It depends on the rest of the sentence in order to make sense.

Editing for Simple and Complex Sentences *(cont.)*

6. Write the following clauses on chart paper. Ask the students to identify whether the clauses are independent or dependent.

   - she bugged them for a year (*independent*)
   - until they finally let her help (*dependent*)
   - I groom and walk pets (*independent*)
   - she takes her work home (*independent*)
   - which is a giant birdcage (*dependent*)
   - for sick and injured birds (*dependent*)
   - the Leemings live on the Indian River (*independent*)
   - for two years (*dependent*)
   - she has trained pups to be guide dogs (*independent*)

7. Have the students complete "Simple or Complex?" on page 143. The students complete the page by determining whether sentences are simple or complex.

8. Continue practice with "Change It!" on page 144. To complete this page, the student adds a dependent clause to each independent clause in order to create a complex sentence.

9. Have each student write a story about a topic of interest, focusing on the use of both simple and complex sentences.

Publication

Have students work together to edit for the use of simple and complex sentences.

Extension

Ask each student to select a previously written story or article to edit for simple and complex sentences. Remind the student to vary sentence length throughout the piece.

Creature Comforter

When Shanin Leeming was in second grade, she asked for a job. She wanted to take care of animals at her local Humane Society shelter. "You're too young," said the shelter workers. But animal-loving Shanin didn't give up. She bugged the staff members for a year, until they finally let her help. "I've worked there ever since," says Shanin, now 13. The American Humane Association appreciates her work so much that the group named her its 1997 National Be Kind to Animals Kid.

"I groom and walk pets, bathe dogs, and train them to make them adoptable," she says. "Kids contact me if they're interested in adopting."

Shanin takes her work home, too. She has cared for many species at her Merrit Island, Florida, house. Her dad helped her build an aviary, which is a giant birdcage, for sick and injured birds. The Leemings live on the Indian River, where Shanin searches by boat for birds in need of help. "I've taken care of peacocks, ducks, sparrows, pigeons, and even a pelican," she says.

Tending to sick animals can be hard work, Shanin says. "It isn't easy getting up in the middle of the night." For two years, she has also trained pups to be guide dogs for the blind.

Sometimes she takes sick animals to school so she can feed them regularly. "I bring them in a small kennel, and they aren't a distraction," says Shanin. Well, there was that day the principal taught a social studies class and Shanin's birds just wouldn't stop screeching!

Shanin has even given up her Christmas presents so the money can go to help animals. "It makes me feel so good," she says. "That's the gift."

Simple or Complex?

Read the following sentences from the article, "Creature Comforter." Beside each sentence, write *S* if the sentence is simple and *C* if it is complex.

_____ 1. Animal-loving Shanin didn't give up.

_____ 2. She bugged the staff members for a year, until they finally let her help.

_____ 3. "Kids contact me if they're interested in adopting."

_____ 4. Shanin takes her work home, too.

_____ 5. Her dad helped her build an aviary, which is a giant birdcage, for sick and injured birds.

_____ 6. The Leemings live on the Indian River, where Shanin searches by boat for birds in need of help.

_____ 7. Tending to sick animals can be hard work.

_____ 8. For two years, she has also trained pups to be guide dogs for the blind.

_____ 9. Shanin has even given up her Christmas presents so the money can go to help animals.

_____ 10. "It makes me feel so good."

Change It!

Rewrite each sentence below to make it complex. Add a dependent clause to each one.

Example: *I was sleepy.*

   When I woke up, I was still sleepy.

1. I got a puppy.

   _____

   _____

2. The tornado destroyed the town.

   _____

   _____

3. I try to stay healthy.

   _____

   _____

4. I saw a great movie.

   _____

   _____

5. We continue to play baseball.

   _____

   _____

6. It rained.

   _____

   _____

7. I am so sad that the art class was cancelled.

   _____

   _____

8. The thunder crashed.

   _____

   _____

Student Writing Sample: The Magic of Christmas

One Christmas Eve I was sleeping on the couch and I heard a bark. Somebody came through the chimney. I saw Santa Claus, the dog. He was giving our three dogs a bone and chew toys.

Then I fell asleep again because somebody else came through the chimney. It was my favorite person, Santa Claus, but somebody was with him. It was Mrs. Claus. While they filled under the tree with presents, I went up the chimney and put the present for them in their sleigh and came back quiet as a mouse.

I lay down and took a drink of water. I fell asleep in an instant. I woke up in the morning. I went and woke my mom and dad. We went to open our presents, but I noticed that our tree wasn't on the ground. It was hovering in the air. I leaped a foot back from the tree!

From then on, I lived happily ever after.

—Breanna H.

Using Quotations Correctly

Objectives

The student will recognize how quotations enhance writing. The student will correctly punctuate quotations.

Skills

- using quotations in writing
- editing for the use of correct punctuation with quotations

Materials

—chart paper

—marker

—"Great Ball of Fire!" (page 148)

—student copies of "May I Quote You?" (page 149)

—writing paper

—pencils

—"Student Writing Sample: My Mean Mom" for teacher reference (page 150)

Procedure

1. Discuss with your students the fact that quotations can enhance written work.

2. Continue the discussion by explaining that an author can tell a story effectively without quotations, but using a person's actual words adds interest and variation to a story.

3. Write the following paragraph on chart paper:

   By understanding what lies beyond the sun's blaze, scientists hope to predict solar weather and its many powerful effects on Earth. They used to think the inside of the sun was simple. Now they can see into the sun and they know that it is more complicated.

4. Now, write the paragraph below on chart paper:

   By understanding what lies beyond the sun's blaze, scientists hope to predict solar weather and its many powerful effects on Earth. "We used to think the inside of the sun was fairly simple," says Arizona astronomer John Harvey. "But that was before we had the capability to see into it."

5. Ask the students to compare the two paragraphs, focusing on the use of quotes, the actual words of a person involved in the story.

6. Explain that using the scientist's words not only adds interest but also makes the story believable because it includes the words of an expert.

7. Have the students take note of the punctuation used with the quotations. Quotation marks surround what is said. A comma separates the quotation from the rest of the sentence.

8. Read "Great Ball of Fire!" and allow the students to discuss the information.

Using Quotations Correctly *(cont.)*

9. Allow your students to practice using correct punctuation with quotations by completing "May I Quote You?" on page 149. The students complete the page by adding quotation marks and commas where needed.

10. Instruct each student to think of a story or an article he or she could write that would include a quote. (See the list below for article ideas.)

   • Food in the Cafeteria
   • Behavior on the Playground
   • Students Who Play Sports
   • The Job of a Librarian
   • The Hardest Thing about Being a Principal
   • My Friend, the Soccer Player
   • Our Family Vacation
   • My Brother's Special Pet

11. The student should plan the article, interview a person related to the story, and then write the story, including a direct quotation.

12. Have each student write his or her story with quotations, paying close attention to the use of correct punctuation.

Publication

1. Divide students into pairs to revise and edit their stories.

2. Instruct the students to read the stories and decide where commas and quotation marks need to be added.

Extension

Have each student select an article or story to read. Instruct the student to locate the use of quotations and note how these sentences create interest.

Great Ball of Fire!

The sun seems to be a quiet neighbor that gives light and heat. It tans sunbathers and helps plants grow. But our nearest star is really a complex, loudly exploding ball of fiery gas. Sometimes it whips up wicked storms on its surface.

This stormy weather can cause big problems here on Earth. Solar storms can make compass needles point the wrong way and can even knock out electric and phone service.

Now scientists are using spacecraft and instruments on Earth to "look inside" the sun. Someday they may be able to forecast solar storms much the way weather forecasters predict rain and snow on Earth.

The *Solar and Heliospheric Observatory* (SOHO) is a spacecraft packed with telescopes. It has been circling the sun, taking pictures and measurements.

Scientists were surprised by SOHO's discoveries, which they announced last month. SOHO found rivers and winds of superhot gas (called plasma) beneath the surface of the sun.

Even more of the sun's secrets will be revealed to scientists. On August 25, 1997, NASA launched the *Advanced Composition Explorer* (ACE). ACE tracks the solar wind—fiery particles of the sun that fly through the solar system and affect weather on the planets.

By understanding what lies beyond the sun's blaze, scientists hope to predict solar weather and its many powerful effects on Earth. "We used to think the inside of the sun was fairly simple," says Arizona astronomer John Harvey. "But that was before we had the capability to see into it."

May I Quote You?

Add correct quotation punctuation to the sentences below.

1. Sammy isn't just a great hitter says Mark Grace. He always plays with a smile. He's fun to be around.

2. Mark is going to break the record Sammy told reporters. He's the man.

3. Venus is so strong and fast says Martina Hingis. I have to play my best against her.

4. I've learned a lot from watching Venus says Serena. Her results have encouraged me to work harder so that I can do well, too.

5. When she is not painting, Alexandra plays with her dog Olive or practices the art of rollerblading. I'm a normal kid first she says. And nothing will ever change that.

6. My grandmother always tells me to do what's right says Larry.

7. For the first 89 days of 1998, there was not a single drop of rain says Smits. It was really a desert climate. Nothing could stand up to that drought.

8. Sometimes it makes you feel desperate he says but we still have to try to help nature, and people, as much as we can.

Student Writing Sample:
My Mean Mom

"Get ready, Courtney and Breanna."

That was the first sound of the morning.

"I'm getting up," said Courtney, my twin sister. "How about you?"

"Yes."

"Breanna, make sure the bacon doesn't burn because you want everything perfect for your mom, right?" said my mom.

"Right," I said, rolling my eyes.

"Don't talk to your sweet mom that way. Today we are going bowling."

"Thank heavens," I said under my breath.

"What did you say?"

"Nothing!" I exclaimed.

—Breanna H.

Enhancing Writing with Charts

Objectives

The student will read charts to locate information. The students will create a chart to enhance writing.

Skills

- understanding the use of charts
- gathering information from charts
- understanding how charts can enhance writing
- creating a tally chart

Materials

—"Champions of the Ice and Snow" (page 153)
—student copies of the article on page 153
—chart paper
—marker
—student copies of "Tally Chart Article" (page 154)
—"Student Writing Sample: Stephanie's Chart" for teacher reference (page 155)

Procedure

1. Explain to your students that charts are used to gather or show different kinds of information.

2. Read "Champions of the Ice and Snow" on page 153. Allow the students to view the chart below the article.

3. Explain that this chart provides information about the number of gold, silver, and bronze medals that were earned in the Olympics by different countries.

4. Distribute student copies of the article and ask the following questions:
   - Which country earned the most medals?
   - Which country earned the least number of medals?
   - Which country earned the most bronze medals?
   - How many more medals did the United States earn than Japan?

5. Draw the students' attention to the format of the chart. The names of the countries are listed along the left side of the chart. The medals are listed across the top. The number of medals is listed in the column below the medal and in the row representing the country.

6. Ask the students to discuss how the chart enhances the article. Does the chart assist the reader in understanding the article? In what way would the article be incomplete without the use of this chart?

7. Explain that a tally chart is another kind of chart that can be used to enhance writing.

Enhancing Writing with Charts *(cont.)*

8. Draw the tally chart below on chart paper.

Favorite Winter Olympic Sport	
Sport	**Tally**
downhill skiing	
figure skating	
ski jumping	
speed skating	
snowboarding	
hockey	
bobsled racing	

9. Ask the students to name their favorites from the chart, one per student. Tally them on the chart as they are named. Draw the students' attention to the use of tally marks to show votes. Explain that the tally marks can be replaced with numbers to make a chart similar to the one in the article.

10. Distribute copies of "Tally Chart Article" on page 154.

11. The students complete the chart and then write an article to accompany it.

12. Finally, ask each student to think of an article topic that can be enhanced by a tally chart. See the list below for ideas.
    - The Worst Cafeteria Lunches
    - The Best Things to Do at Recess
    - Which is better—P.E. or art?
    - Things Our Teacher Hates

13. Have each student survey the class, create a tally chart displaying the information, and write an article about the topic.

Publication

1. Display the students' articles and charts for all to see.

2. Have each student create a list of questions to answer using the chart. Display the list beside his or her chart.

Extension

1. Allow the students to recreate their charts using a word-processing program. To do this, open a new document. From the top menu, click on Table and select Insert Table. In the resulting window, select the desired number of columns and rows and then click OK. A table will appear on the document. The table can be labeled with the information for the chart.

2. Ask students to create tally charts to display information from home, such as the number of hours spent watching television during the week or the family's favorite foods.

Champions of the Ice and Snow

A dream came true for the U.S. women's hockey team. The women beat Canada and won the first Olympic gold medal ever given in women's hockey.

Later, U.S. figure skater Tara Lipinski, 15, wore the biggest grin of all. She leaped past Michelle Kwan to win the gold medal. She is the youngest Olympic figure-skating champion ever.

The power of hockey and the beauty of skating were just two of the wonders seen at the 1998 Winter Games in Nagano (Nah-gah-no), Japan. Heavy snows delayed many events. But the wait was worth it!

U.S. skier Picabo Street smashed her knee a year ago. She won gold in Nagano.

The U.S. earned two medals in snowboarding, a new Olympic sport. In the sledding sport called luge, Americans won medals for the first time. "We're not Michael Jordans," said luger Gordy Sheer. "But I hope this brings some awareness to our sport."

Athletes set many new records on the ice and snow. Speed skaters broke at least six world and 12 Olympic records!

Cross-country skier Bjorn Dahlie (Be-orn Day-lee) of Norway won his seventh gold. That brought his Olympic-medal total to 11 (in three Games)—the most for any Winter Olympian.

The sound of 2,000 drums brought the Games to an end. Some 200 athletes carried home medals. All left with Olympic memories.

Skating for the gold was "pure joy," said Lipinski. "I will always remember it."

The Medal Count

What country won the most Olympic medals in Nagano? Countries with chilly climates came out on top. Here are the medal totals as of 2/20/98:

Country	Gold	Silver	Bronze	Total
1. Germany	10	9	8	27
2. Norway	8	8	5	21
3. Russia	9	5	2	16
4. Austria	3	5	7	15
5. Canada	5	5	4	14
6. United States	6	3	4	13
7. Netherlands	5	4	2	11
8. Finland	2	4	5	11
9. Italy	2	6	2	10
10. Japan	4	1	3	8

Tally Chart Article

Select a topic for a class survey, such as favorite books or favorite school lunches. Create a tally chart in the box below. Then write an article to go along with the chart.

Article Title: _____

Chart Title: _____

Choices	Tally Marks

Student Writing Sample: Stephanie's Chart

Stephanie wanted to see if she had enough time to get to the library before it closed. But she had other errands she had to do first. She asked her mother for advice, and she told her to make a chart. Stephanie thought that was a great idea! Here is the chart she made:

Library Closes = 8:00 P.M.   Leaving Time = 7:00 P.M.

Destinations					Approximate Minutes Needed
Betty's House	Bank	Post Office	Video Store	Library	
■	■	■	■	■	5 minutes
■	■		■	■	10 minutes
■	■				15 minutes
	■				20 minutes
					25 minutes
					30 minutes
					35 minutes
					Total minutes = exactly one hour!

"Goody," said Stephanie aloud. "I can make it! These chart things are pretty cool. I'll have to use them more often."

—*Annie H.*

Enhancing Writing with Graphs

Objectives

The student will read vertical and horizontal bar graphs. The student will recognize how graphs enhance writing. The student will create a bar graph to accompany a piece of writing.

Skills

- reading graphs
- gathering information from graphs
- creating graphs

Materials

—"Top 5 Graphs" (page 158)

—student copies of "More Top 5 Graphs" (page 159)

—student copies of "Reading Bar Graphs" (page 160)

—student copies of "Making Bar Graphs" (page 161)

—"Student Writing Sample: Pet Graph" for teacher reference (page 162)

Procedure

1. Explain to the students that articles often include visual aids to provide more information and/or interest. Visual aids can come in the form of illustrations, photographs, diagrams, charts, maps, and graphs.

2. Tell the students that the article for this lesson includes a graph.

3. Read aloud "Top 5 Graphs" on page 158. Allow the students to discuss the article.

4. Then tell the students that they will have the opportunity to take a closer look at the graph included in the article.

5. Distribute copies of "More Top 5 Graphs" on page 159.

6. Explain to the students that the graphs on this page are bar graphs. Some bar graphs are vertical and some are horizontal.

7. Explain that by looking at the graphs it is easy to see which fruits and vegetables were the favorites of Americans in 1996. A closer look tells us specific information about the number of vegetables and fruits eaten, but a quick glance provides information as well.

8. Instruct the students to complete the page by using the graphs to answer questions.

9. Continue the discussion about the article by asking the following questions:

   - How do the graphs enhance the article?
   - What information do the graphs provide that the article does not?
   - Do you think the article would be as interesting without the graphs?

Enhancing Writing with Graphs *(cont.)*

10. Next, spend time focusing on the specific components of a graph. Explain that graphs have columns and rows. They also have titles and labels.

11. Distribute copies of "Reading Bar Graphs" on page 160. Ask the students to locate the title, column, and row labels.

12. Ask the students to take note of the information on both graphs. The information is the same, but the graphs are different—one is vertical and one is horizontal.

13. Review with the students how to read the graph to determine the number of children who like certain pets.

14. Challenge the students further by having them create graphs of their own, using information provided on "Making Bar Graphs" (page 161).

15. Ask the students to think of ways that bar graphs can be used in written work.

Publication

Instruct each student to think of a topic of interest that could include a graph. (The student may want to conduct a survey in order to gather information for the graph.) Each student writes an article, creates an accompanying graph, and displays the two together.

Extension

1. Show the students a magazine or newspaper article containing a bar graph. Read all or some of the article and allow them to view and discuss the graph.

2. On a bulletin board, display a large bar graph. Attach question cards (pertaining to the graph) to the bulletin board around the graph. Encourage the students to read the graph and determine the answers.

3. As an additional activity, have the students create graphs by using a spreadsheet program, such as *Microsoft Excel*. To make a graph of daily temperatures, a student types a day of the week in a cell of the spreadsheet and then types the temperature in the cell below it. The student clicks on the graph feature (usually located in the menu at the top of the screen). The graph tool will guide the student through the process of making different kinds of graphs. The student will be able to choose to make a bar graph, a line graph, or even a pie graph.

Top 5 Graphs

Do you think broccoli tastes bitter? Don't blame the cook! Researchers have announced that what tastes good or bad can depend on the taster's genes. Genes are the chemical instructions that make you who you are. They determine the color of your eyes and the shape of your nose and face. Now scientists know that they also determine how many taste buds are on your tongue.

One-quarter of people arc supertasters. They have so many taste buds that they find the flavor of some foods unpleasantly strong. Cabbage seems very bitter to them, while chocolate seems way too sweet. One-quarter are nontasters with few taste buds. Half are medium tasters who enjoy most foods.

Top 5 Vegetables

Don't use your genes as an excuse to skip your veggies! For vitamins and other nutrients, vegetables are always in good taste. The graph below shows how much of the five favorite vegetables an average American eats each year.

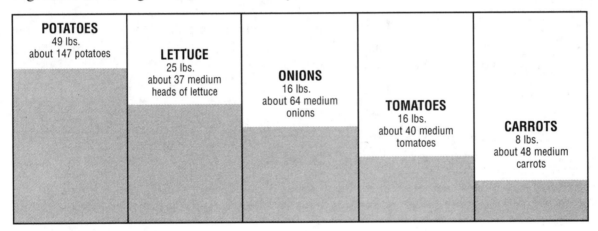

Top 5 Fruits

Watermelons, peaches, plums: summer is the season for fruit. But pound for pound, bananas are the most a-peeling. The graph below shows how many of these juicy favorites the average American eats in one year.

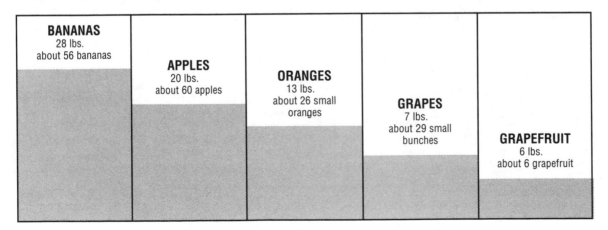

More Top 5 Graphs

Use the graphs on page 158 to answer the questions below.

1. Are these graphs vertical or horizontal? _____

2. What is the favorite fruit? _____

3. What is the favorite vegetable? _____

4. Do people eat more onions or carrots? _____

5. Do people eat fewer oranges or grapes? _____

6. How many pounds of lettuce do people eat each year? _____

7. How many more pounds of tomatoes are eaten than carrots? _____

Reading Bar Graphs

Use the graphs below to answer the questions.

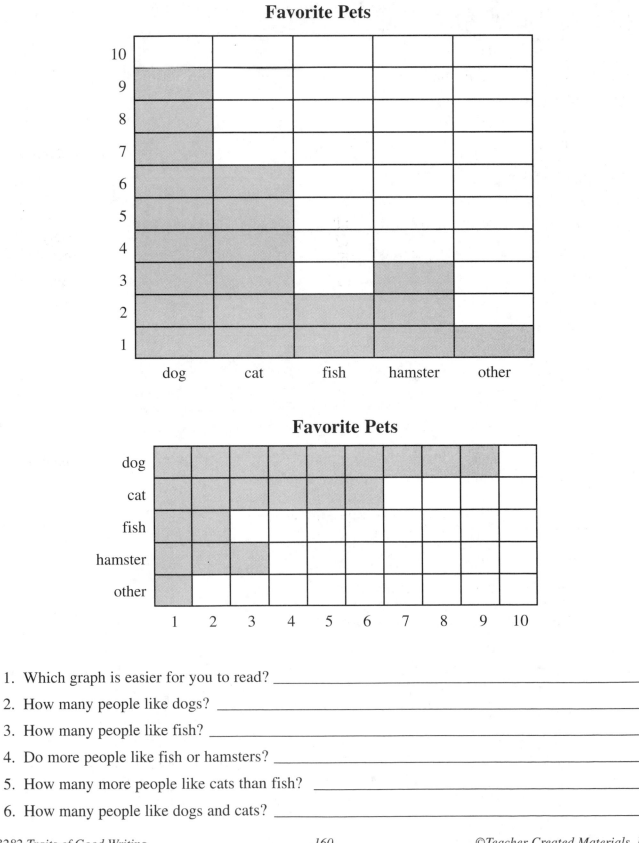

Favorite Pets

Favorite Pets

1. Which graph is easier for you to read? _____

2. How many people like dogs? _____

3. How many people like fish? _____

4. Do more people like fish or hamsters? _____

5. How many more people like cats than fish? _____

6. How many people like dogs and cats? _____

Making Bar Graphs

Use the information below to create a bar graph. Be sure to label the graph and include a title.

Favorite Wild Animals

- lions = 4
- bears = 2
- alligators = 3
- jaguars = 10
- giraffes = 4
- hippos = 1

Student Writing Sample:
Pet Graph

Here is a graph of all my pets. I have six pets in all.

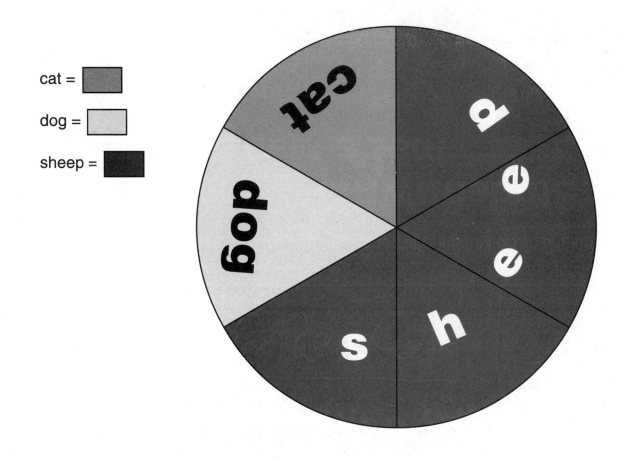

Four of my animals are sheep. One is a cat. One is a dog. I enjoy all of them very much. I use the sheep for 4-H. In fact, one of the ewes (mother sheep) has just recently had a lamb.

Animals are a very neat part of God's creation.

—Stuart R.

Making Picture Diagrams

Objective

The student will identify the usefulness of picture diagrams and make his or her own.

Skills

- identifying the purpose of picture diagrams
- identifying the labels of a diagram
- writing or selecting a story that can be enhanced by a diagram
- making a picture diagram

Materials

—"Tornado Watch: Tracking Storms" (page 165)

—student copies of page 165

—student copies of "Picture Diagram" (page 166)

—chart paper

—marker

—"Student Writing Sample: Inez's Map" for teacher reference (page 167)

—water cycle reference books (optional)

Procedure

1. Explain to the students that diagrams are often useful additions to articles.

2. A picture diagram can make the topic of an article easier to understand.

3. Distribute copies of "Tornado Watch: Tracking Storms" on page 165.

4. Discuss the picture diagram used in the article. Ask the following questions:
   - What does the diagram show?
   - Does the diagram capture your attention?
   - Can you tell what the article is about by looking at the diagram?
   - What information does the diagram provide about tornadoes?

5. Explain that a picture diagram can show many things. See the list below for examples:
   - the parts of a flower
   - the positions of players on a baseball field
   - the arrangement of books in a library
   - the parts of a human skeleton
   - the structure of a spaceship

6. In this article, the diagram shows the parts of a tornado. Seeing this diagram gives the reader a better understanding of a tornado.

7. Have the students read the article or read it together as a class.

Making Picture Diagrams *(cont.)*

8. Provide each student with a copy of the diagram on page 166.

9. Have the students complete their pages by using a reference book (if necessary) to determine the location of each label in the Word Box.

10. Ask the students to take note of the parts of the diagram and how they are labeled.

11. Explain that a diagram is not just a picture. It has labels to identify the parts of the item being shown.

12. As a class, create a diagram of your school cafeteria. Have the students think about how a diagram of the cafeteria might help a new student on the first day at your school. Invite the students to tell the things that would be important to include in the diagram, such as the following:

    • the line for getting hot lunch
    • where to pay for lunch
    • the location of the class lunch table
    • the location of the bathrooms
    • the location of the door that leads to the playground

13. Draw the diagram on chart paper and have the students dictate the labels that should be added as you write them on the diagram.

14. Ask each student to write an article or select a piece of written work from his or her writing portfolio that can be enhanced with a diagram.

15. Instruct each student to draw and label a picture diagram relating to the topic of his or her article.

Publication

1. Invite each student to share his or her article and the related diagram. Have the student explain how the diagram enhances the article and the information it provides to the reader. Invite other students to comment on the diagram and share how the use of the diagram was helpful in better understanding the article.

2. Display the students' articles and diagrams on a bulletin board entitled "Picture This!"

Extension

1. Allow the students to create word-processed labels for their diagrams. Encourage them to adjust fonts and point sizes to create visual appeal.

2. Allow the students to create diagrams using your classroom computer. The students may want to use the drawing feature of a word-processing program. The students may also want to select clip art from the program and then add labels of these already created diagrams.

3. Distribute copies of newspapers or social studies or science magazines. Have the students look for articles that contain picture diagrams. Have the students respond to these articles by explaining how the diagrams made the articles more interesting or meaningful.

Tornado Watch: Tracking Storms

The chase was on. Mark Askelson was riding in a speeding truck. Danger was rushing closer and closer: a swirling, angry tornado. Askelson had to get to safety. But it wasn't time for him to get out of the storm's way—yet.

First he had to drop tools in the path of the tornado. The tools would measure the storm's temperature and strength. Askelson placed the tools and then quickly found safety.

Askelson works for the National Severe Storms Laboratory in Norman, Oklahoma. He studies tornadoes to figure out when and where they will hit. With that information, scientists can give people warning. "That's our goal: to answer scientific questions about tornadoes so that we can help save people's lives," says Askelson.

Tornadoes are nature's most powerful storms. They can produce super strong winds that blow at speeds of 300 miles an hour. When a tornado strikes, it can cause a lot of serious damage.

Spring is tornado season in the South. In April 1998, tornadoes struck eight states in the Southeast. That season's storms were especially deadly. They hit more cities and towns than usual. The tornadoes killed 112 people.

Rodney Standford of Nashville, Tennessee, saw a twister tear through a football stadium. "Parts of the stadium were being tossed around like Popsicle sticks," he said. "I've never seen anything like it."

Scientists are a long way from knowing how to stop tornadoes. But they're closer than ever to understanding why they form. (See the box below.) Says Askelson, "We're moving toward a time when we'll be able to give people hours of notice before a storm hits." Those hours will save lives.

A giant storm system made of moisture and wind is called a supercell. It is formed when warm air crashes into cooler air. The crash sometimes causes the wind to start spinning and form a tornado. The center of a tornado is called a vortex. Most tornadoes are black from dust and dirt they suck up from the ground.

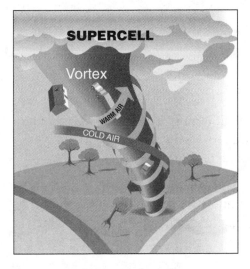

SUPERCELL
Vortex
WARM AIR
COLD AIR

Picture Diagram

Complete the diagram by labeling each part of the water cycle, using the words from the Word Box. You may use others sources to help, if needed.

The Water Cycle

1. _____

2. _____

3. _____

Word Box

condensation

precipitation

evaporation

Student Writing Sample: Inez's Map

So many places to go, so little time. That's how Inez felt. She needed to find the quickest route to where she was going. So, she drew a map.

Inez figured out the quickest route with her map. Then she was able to run her errands along the quickest route.

—*Misha T.*

Illustrations and Page Layout

Objectives

The student will determine the best items to illustrate in his or her written work. The student will create illustrations to accompany his or her writing.

Skills

- identifying the effectiveness of illustrations and photographs
- determining the best things to illustrate
- drawing appropriate illustrations

Materials

—an interesting article with illustrations from a magazine or newspaper

—copies of the article for small groups of students to share

—student copies of "Get the Picture?" (page 169)

—student copies of "Article Template" (page 170)

—"Writing Sample Format Ideas" for teacher reference (page 171)

Procedure

1. Read aloud the selected article.

2. Show the students the illustrations used to accompany the article. (You may want to duplicate a few extra copies of the article and have the students look at the pictures in small groups.)

3. Draw the students' attention to the use of the illustrations. What do they show? How do these illustrations enhance the article? Have the students take note of the way the illustrations are placed on the page. Explain that the position of the illustrations is almost as important as the illustrations themselves.

4. Explain that when illustrating an article, it is only necessary to select a few pieces of information to show.

5. Ask each student to select an article from his or her writing portfolio.

6. Distribute copies of "Get the Picture?" on page 169. The student should read his or her article and use the worksheet to select information to illustrate and plan the illustrations.

Publication

Have the students rewrite their articles, using one or two illustrations placed in visually appealing locations on the paper. Distribute copies of the article template on page 170 to help.

Extension

1. Instruct the students to find additional magazine or newspaper articles that utilize illustrations in eye-catching ways.

2. Make a bulletin board of magazine/newspaper articles (containing illustrations) to serve as inspiration for future page layouts.

Get the Picture?

Read the article you wrote and determine what information could be enhanced with illustrations. Write two pieces of information on the lines below. In the boxes, sketch ideas for your illustrations to accompany the information you selected.

Information #1:

_____

_____

Information: #2:

_____

_____

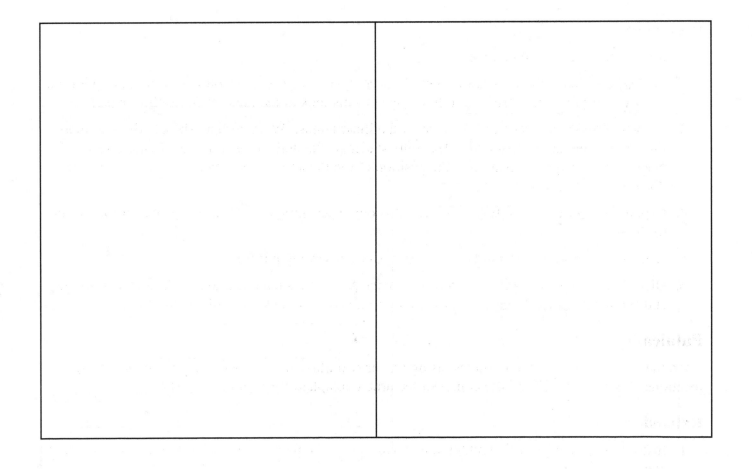

Article Template

Write your article on the lines below. Draw two appropriate illustrations in the boxes.

Writing Sample Format Ideas

Here are some templates of different design layouts.

(illustration)

_____

(illustration)

(illustration)

(illustration)

(illustration)

(illustration)

(illustration)

Answer Key

Page 24

1. Rewrites will vary.
2. yes
3. yes
4. Rewrites will vary.
5. Rewrites will vary.
6. Rewrites will vary.
7. yes
8. Rewrites will vary.

Page 30

Beginning

I heard a fire engine.

I smelled smoke.

A fireman said we had to leave.

Middle

The building next door was on fire.

The firemen were spraying water on our roof.

Mom called my sister.

End

Everyone got out safely.

Some people lost everything.

We put new smoke alarms in the apartment.

Page 36

1. A
2. B or C
3. B or D
4. C
5. B or C

Page 59

1. E
2. N
3. N
4. E
5. E
6. N

Page 70

1. The author thinks the president should spend more money on public schools.
2. Things that will change with increased education include the following: "boost the economy, prevent homelessness, help stop the spread of AIDS, and help save the environment."
3. Answers will vary.
4. Answers will vary.

Page 71

1. persuading
2. persuading
3. telling
4. persuading
5. telling
6. telling
7. telling
8. persuading

Answer Key *(cont.)*

Page 78

1. nibbled
2. tiptoed
3. stomped
4. gobbled
5. glanced
6. stared
7. paced
8. gazed
9. devoured
10. strolled
11. roared
12. whispered
13. cried
14. sighed

Page 103

1. sit down and rest
2. made me very sad
3. teasing/joking with me
4. watch
5. do not speak
6. rely on
7. raining heavily
8. completely still
9. voraciously (a great deal)
10. sick
11. behave in a silly way
12. a great deal of money

Page 115

1. The cat curled up on the cushion and cried.
2. One Saturday a silly snake slithered in the sand.
3. Two tiny turtles trotted to the town.
4. The winter wind whipped past the water.
5. The pitter patter poured down on the pavement.
6. The bear ate berries for a breakfast.

Page 120

Answers will vary according to the dictionary used.

Page 121

1. sleek
2. lunar
3. agency
4. astronauts
5. surface
6. guidelines
7. exploration
8. weight
9. antenna
10. eventually
11. astronomers
12. comets
13. citizens

Page 126

Main Ideas

1. So scientists are inventing ways of making spider silk without spiders.
2. Finding new planets is no easy job.
3. But today more archaelogists than ever are turning their attention to ancient Nubia, the world's first known black civilization.

Answer Key *(cont.)*

Page 132

The correct punctuation is embedded within the paragraph.

Have you ever been boating on a river? You would expect to see clear water, fish, birds, and healthy plants. Let me tell you about my trip down our local river.

I saw a refrigerator, a dead cow, and soda pop cans. I saw plastic cups, sewer pipes, and dirty water. I didn't enjoy this trip. There was too much pollution in the river.

I feel the president should make cleaning up our waterways one of the first things he does. He should do this because we drink water from this river and other rivers like it. We need water. We need it to be clean. We can get sick from dirty water and die.

I would like to see our rivers cleaned up. This would give us clean drinking water and a great place to fish. This could be done by removing the trash and waste products. Then we would make sure that they do not get put back into the river. Maybe our laws could be more strict. People would think before they polluted our rivers.

When I grow up, I want to bring my son down the river. I want him to see only fish, birds, clean water, and green plants. Wouldn't it be nice if he could also take a drink?

Page 137

Names of Months: October, April

Names of Countries/Cities: Lisburn, Northern Ireland, England, Britain, Irish Republic

A Person's Title: U.S. Senator, President

Names of People: Laura Lesley, George Mitchell, Clinton

Names of Religions: Catholic, Protestant

Page 138

Words to capitalize:

Atlantic Ocean (1 time)

Canada (1 time)

Free Willy (1 time)

Free Willy Keiko Foundation (1 time)

Hollywood (1 time)

Iceland (3 times)

Keiko (4 times)

Keiko's (2 times)

Mexico (3 times)

Newport, Oregon (1 time)

North Atlantic Ocean (1 time)

Page 143

1. S
2. C
3. S
4. S
5. C
6. C
7. S
8. C
9. C
10. S

Page 149

The correct quotation punctuation is embedded within the paragraph.

1. "Sammy isn't just a great hitter," says Mark Grace. "He always plays with a smile. He's fun to be around."

2. "Mark is going to break the record," Sammy told reporters. "He's the man."

3. "Venus is so strong and fast," says Martina Hingis. "I have to play my best against her."

Answer Key *(cont.)*

Page 149 *(cont.)*

4. "I've learned a lot from watching Venus," says Serena. "Her results have encouraged me to work harder so that I can do well, too."

5. When she is not painting, Alexandra plays with her dog Olive or practices the art of rollerblading. "I'm a normal kid first," she says. And nothing will ever change that.

6. "My grandmother always tells me to do what's right," says Larry.

7. "For the first 89 days of 1998, there was not a single drop of rain," says Smits. "It was really a desert climate. Nothing could stand up to that drought."

8. "Sometimes it makes you feel desperate," he says, "but we still have to try to help nature, and people, as much as we can."

Page 159

1. vertical
2. bananas
3. potatoes
4. onions
5. grapes
6. 25 pounds
7. 8 pounds

Page 160

1. answers will vary
2. nine
3. two
4. hamsters
5. four more
6. 15

Page 166

1. condensation (clouds form)
2. precipitation (rain falls)
3. evaporation (vapor rises)

Skills Matrix